Trickle-Down
MORALITY

*Returning to Truth
in a World of Compromise*

Don S. Otis

Chosen Books

A Division of Baker Book House Co
Grand Rapids, Michigan 49516

Published by Chosen Books
A division of Baker Book House Company
P.O. Box 6287, Grand Rapids, MI 49516-6287

Second printing, August 1998

Printed in the United States of America

Library of Congress Cataloging-in-Publication Data

Otis, Don S., 1956–
    Trickle-down morality : returning to truth in a world of compromise / Don S. Otis.
        p.   cm.
    Includes bibliographical references (p.   ) and index.
    ISBN 0-8007-9257-2 (pbk.)
    1. Hypocrisy—Religious aspects—Christianity. 2. Self-deception—Religious aspects—Christianity. I. Title.
BV4627.H8085   1998
241'.673—dc21   97-38084

For current information about all releases from Baker Book House, visit our web site:
                    http://www.bakerbooks.com

Contents

Acknowledgments

I want to thank my mother, who has been an example of selflessness as long as I can remember; my father, who has provided inspiration and encouragement; and my wife, Susan, who has put up with my theorizing, analyzing and deliberating about the topic of self-deception for nearly a dozen years. I want to thank Jane Campbell, my editor, who is not only a gifted editor but a godly and trusted friend. People like Pastor Jack Stiles of Osborne Neighborhood Church have shown me that character and humility are virtues too undervalued today. I am grateful to my Sunday school class at Sandpoint Assembly of God. They have allowed me to articulate many of the ideas in the following chapters.

Finally I have been influenced by the writing of, and in some instances personal conversations with, Gordon MacDonald, Jack Hayford, Chuck Colson, Richard Dobbins, David Wilkerson and Francis Schaeffer.

Introduction

Twelve-year-old Jeff Maier became an instant hero, except to Baltimore Orioles fans. His picture appeared in every major newspaper from New York to Los Angeles. How exactly did Maier become a hero? A Little League pitcher watching the major league playoffs from the right-field stands, Jeff stuck his gloved left hand over the fence during a tight game between the Orioles and the New York Yankees. He caught a ball hit by a Yankee slugger that would probably have been an out. Instead it was erroneously ruled a home run. "As a Yankee fan," said Maier, "if I helped the team, I feel pretty good. I think I had the right to catch it." The following day he played hooky from school to make whirlwind appearances on *Good Morning, America, Geraldo* and *Hard Copy*.

At first, like any other sports fan, I was amused by Maier's story. But the all-American boy dressed in Yankee pinstripes and a wide grin did not tell the whole story. He did not plan to spoil the game for Orioles fans. But the national response struck me as peculiar. Maier broke the rules. He reached in to deflect a baseball in play—clearly against the rules—and the Orioles eventually lost the game in extra innings. I began to think about what would happen if, instead of being treated as a hero, Maier was fined for interfering in the game. But that did not happen.

Do our choices really matter to God or to others? Do these choices have any meaningful impact on our social environment or culture? Even more important, how do good people rationalize or justify the choices they make that are wrong? In Maier's case, few of us (unless we are Orioles fans) saw anything wrong with his actions. As we will see in the course of this book, however, the primary ingredient in living moral lives is to embrace the biblical concept of truth. Not just anyone's interpretation of the truth, but one based on biblical realities that supersede our own. Fortunately, biblical truth and absolutes are not ambiguous.

And our personal choices do make a difference. The sum of our choices, good or bad, determine who we really are. They form our character. They define us from the inside out. The development and nurturing of moral character in children or adults begin one decision at a time. And good moral reasoning leading to good choices rarely comes without personal cost.

As we search for answers to moral malaise, we must not forget that corporate morality stems from the collective choices individuals make one at a time. During a time when questionable ethics and poor decisions are given a hero's reward, you and I must risk being misunderstood for doing what is right. We must make moral course corrections when these are needed, and hold the line against moral decay in our churches (and in ourselves) even before we try to correct those within our society.

As ancient Israel's King Ahab prepared for battle, the ungodly king scolded God's prophet with these words: "How many times must I make you swear to tell me nothing but the truth in the name of the LORD?" (2 Chronicles 18:15). A variation of these words is asked in our courts: "Do you swear to tell the truth, the whole truth and nothing but the truth, so help you God?" This thing called truth is the glue that holds our social relationships together— and ultimately our society. There is nowhere truth should be guarded more than among those who claim to serve God.

I am sorry to say that this is not always the case. As you will see throughout this book, subtle deviations from moral truth and honesty weaken our walk with God and damage our relationships. The good news is that openness and honesty about ourselves will bring lasting change.

Don S. Otis
Sandpoint, Idaho

PART 1

Trickle-Down Morality

Nothing but the Truth

Our society finds truth too strong a medicine to digest undiluted. In its purest form truth is not a polite tap on the shoulder; it is a howling reproach.

Ted Koppel

To lie a little is not possible. Whoever lies, lies a whole lie.

Victor Hugo, *Les Misérables*

The first ten years of their marriage were like riding an emotional roller coaster. On Sundays Carl and Mary got up early and dressed their three children for church, where Carl was a respected Sunday school teacher. But at home after church, when Carl did not get his way, he flew into a rage. He was not the mild-mannered, godly man other Christians thought he was.

Mary had grown up in a loving home in which she never had to deal with the kind of anger Carl expressed. She was unprepared for how to cope with an abusive husband. Nor were there textbooks back then for abused wives. "It is something you never forget," she says.

Mary admits her husband was a nice guy who loved his kids and worked hard to provide for their needs. But Carl's Jekyll-and-Hyde personality kept family members on edge.

He could not control his temper. When Mary did something he did not like, Carl slapped her hard, even though he feared, with her eyes blackened from abuse, that his secret would be uncovered and his good reputation tarnished. "He knew it was wrong," says Mary, "but he kept doing it for ten years. He knew what he should be doing, but he wasn't doing it."

Today Mary says her late husband struggled constantly with his spiritual life. Although on the outside he was a model Christian, Carl was a religious hypocrite.

In any sizable group of Christians today are tax cheaters, abusers, liars and those addicted to prescription drugs, alcohol or pornography. This reality is dismissed by those who say, "We are all sinners." We are, of course: "All have sinned and fall short of the glory of God" (Romans 3:23). But I object to passive acceptance of behavior like Carl's abuse. We cannot excuse his actions by simply labeling him a sinner.

Even so, this is not the full story. While many pundits decry the secularization of our culture, I believe we have missed the most important ingredient. It is not liberalism, secularism, pluralism (which breeds tolerance) or moral revisionism that is the problem. These are all symptomatic of something bigger—a far greater evil. Our moral ills breed in a climate of individual excuse-making, compromise and justification. Individual choices, often small choices, taken in their totality equal corporate or societal behavior. These choices become the norms by which we govern our lives. We cannot honestly expect to fix the moral ills of a society whose individual members are not making wise moral decisions in their own lives.

The place to begin our quest for moral renewal is with ourselves—often (if not always) in cases like Mary and Carl's, where to protect our sense of morality, we rationalize sinful behavior.

Instead of taking responsibility for his abusive behavior, Carl always found a way to blame his wife. If he was angry, she must have done something to set him off. "Everything I did was criticized," says Mary. "I couldn't pray right. I never looked right. I never did anything right. It took me 23 years to figure out I wasn't all wrong."

Mary eventually did about the only thing she could do: She left him.

No one could understand her decision, of course, least of all those "good" Christians in her church. "People in my church ignored me," says Mary. Even when they found out Carl was abusing Mary, some felt she was at fault. Others refused to believe her side of the story. Still others were quick to point out her biblical duty to support her husband, even if it meant her own demise.

Giving Ourselves a Break

This book is about how we rationalize behavior and moral choices for the sake of personal expedience or comfort or gain. The term *rationalization* means to cause something to appear reasonable, to attribute one's actions to rational or credible motives without analyzing true or unconscious motives. We can and sometimes do rationalize in both big and small ways.

We may employ rationalization, for example, to escape a dinner date with someone we do not want to spend time with, so we create an excuse—and compromise truth. A Christian waitress who refuses to report her tips at tax time might reason, *My wages are too low. If I report everything I earn, I might have to go on government assistance. By not reporting it, I'm actually saving the government money.* Then there is the evangelist who watches an X-rated program on his hotel television. *Maybe it'll help my sex life,* he reasons. We use company phones, copy machines and office supplies, and we take overly long lunch breaks. The excuses are endless: "I'm underpaid." "I deserve better treatment." "Everyone else does the same."

Physician Keith Ablow offered a peek in *U.S. News & World Report* at how we compromise in small ways:

> We give ourselves breaks, a few too many items in the [express] check-out at the grocery store, a few padded expense vouchers for income tax time, a little fib about our car for sale, just one extramarital affair. No one will get hurt. We're human, aren't we?[1]

But we are paying the price for our carefree attitudes. Although we might wink at the "little things," they pave the way for more serious sins.

Rationalization is a form of self-deception. We try to convince ourselves that something wrong is really O.K. But we are lying to ourselves, twisting the truth to make a wrong choice appear more acceptable.

Consider the man who stops to look at a beautiful red car parked in front of a dealership. Once lured into the showroom, he looks at the sticker on the window and realizes he made a mistake even bothering to stop. But the determined salesman convinces him to take a test drive. "Don't worry," he says, "there's no obligation." By the time they arrive back at the dealership, they are already talking about how much his trade-in is worth and what the monthly payments will be. He is hooked. Our friend drives home in a new car that he will be paying for over the next 72 months!

On his way home, he realizes he has some explaining to do to his wife. But by the time he pulls into the driveway, he is ready for her barrage of questions. When she exclaims, "What in the world have you done?", he replies, "Honey, you know how badly we needed a new car and the mileage we have on the old one. Besides, they gave me such a good deal."

The human penchant for rationalization is infinite. We are forever trying to affirm ourselves. But this habit is dangerous. When we carry it into the moral compartments of our lives, it can damage our moral gyroscopes.

Today moral absolutes no longer guide the behavior of most people. Our society is far more concerned with personal rights than with personal responsibilities. We are surrounded by a secular culture vying for our moral sympathies. The Church, sad to say, is giving in to the pressure for compromise. A 1994 report by the Barna Research Group found that four out of ten people who call themselves born again do not believe in such a thing as absolute truth.[2] An earlier study by the Princeton Religion Research Center found a higher percentage (45 percent) of evangelicals reporting that they rely more on themselves to solve the problems of life than on an outside power such as God.[3]

On Sunday mornings we sing about victory in Jesus, but a brief menagerie of recent media headlines about Christians attests to the moral slippage within the Church: *Adultery Muzzles Careers of Singers; $1.75 Million Paid to Abuse Victims; Adultery, Financial Mismanagement Accusations Leveled against Ministry of "Biker Pastor"; Episcopal Bishop Ordains Lesbian into Priesthood; Alcohol Bedevils Many in Clergy; Women Charge [Minister] with Abuse.* If you read these headlines and assume they are merely the result of man's fallenness, you will miss the overall thrust of this book.

What *is* the thrust of this book? That rationalization leads to self-deception, in ourselves and in others—and self-deception may be the most underrated problem facing the Church today.

How We Come to Deceive Ourselves

The word *deceive* means to ensnare or fool. Throughout this book, the term *deception* refers to the person who has compromised his or her behavior to accommodate either conscience or activities. It is accepting actions or ways of thinking that are wrong; lying to oneself for the sake of expediency.

It is not just that many of us who name the name of Jesus call right wrong or wrong right. We have also learned, in subtle and often indiscernible ways, to accept behavior in ourselves and others that runs counter to the truth of God's Word. My emphasis in this book, then, is not simply on those who sin. The Bible makes it clear we *all* have fallen short of God's design. My concern includes the casual attitude many of us have toward the habitual violation of God's Word.

Self-deception begins with a decision to compromise absolute truth. It often begins with a half-truth, since half-truths do not seem as bad to our moral sensibilities.

Consider the wife who arrives home late from an outing to the dentist, the department store and the grocery store. Last night she and her husband discussed how tight their household budget was and agreed not to buy anything unnecessary for a couple of months. Yet on her way home from the dentist this afternoon, she spotted a department store banner reading *Today Only, 50% Off*. She left the store with bags full of purchases. Now, as she arrives home, her husband says, "I was worried about you. Where have you been?" She responds, "Honey, you knew I'd be at the dentist this afternoon." Then she proceeds to tell him about her dental checkup and asks for help with the groceries.

The wife's response is not a direct lie. It is a half-truth. She has selectively left out important details about where she has been, intending to deceive her husband and deflect further accountability. (Explaining the purchases that show up on the credit card in a few weeks will be her next challenge!)

Whenever we make excuses for behavior we know is wrong, we are engaging in self-deception. In our attempt to appease our consciences, we affix labels to our wrong behavior. We refer to immoral movies or videos as "educational" or "entertaining." We call certain lies "white lies" or say, "I was only joking."

What happens when these excuses translate into a lifestyle of compromise? Eventually we become unable to tell the difference between complete truth and our own made-up "reality." We make decisions (often on the spur of the moment) that serve our immediate interests, and feel no remorse. The Bible refers to a conscience "seared with a hot iron" (1 Timothy 4:2, KJV), and this is what self-deception is all about. Eventually those within the Church cease to be effective purveyors of truth. Instead we find ourselves leaking the same moral sewage that flows in the gutters of secularism.

Who Are the Deceivers?

When you think of the biblical warnings about the last days, what comes to mind? Do you think of earthquakes, famines, wars and lawlessness? You might find it interesting to learn there is one common thread about the end times that weaves its way through Scripture: the admonition against falling prey to deception and deceivers. The first and last warnings about the end times in Jesus' discourse on the Mount of Olives are cautions about deception. Jesus started by saying, "Watch out that no one deceives you" (Matthew 24:4), and concluded with a warning about false prophets who "will appear and perform great signs and miracles to deceive even the elect—if that were possible" (verse 24). In this discourse Jesus used the word *deceive* four different times. The apostle Paul added that "[Satan's] servants masquerade as servants of righteousness" (2 Corinthians 11:15).

At first glance the references to false prophets might seem irrelevant to you. But if a deceiver or false prophet is anyone who portrays the truth of God falsely, it looks different. Could a false prophet be someone who convinces us it is O.K. to divorce a spouse, go to a filthy movie or lie to an employer? This broader definition of *false prophet*—one I believe is accurate—sweeps far more of us into it.

Let me illustrate. Justin, my oldest son, spent the night at a friend's house when he was nine. We found out that his friend's parents had X-rated cable programs running while he was there. He has not been allowed back since! But suppose Justin had said, "I don't feel comfortable with the program you're watching." And suppose, in response, that his friend's parents had sat him down and said, "Justin, there is nothing wrong with sex. You should not be ashamed of viewing the human body. Your parents are trying to inhibit your personal growth. It's time for you to grow up." As a parent I would be understandably upset. Someone would be trying to undermine the values I have been teaching my son.

In that very way, a false prophet can be anyone who gives advice or encourages us to act against the will of God; someone who brings into question the absoluteness or completeness of God's Word. He undermines the Lawgiver by creating doubt about certain moral realities. He or she is a deceiver.

I have brought false prophets into the discussion of self-deception because we face at least three serious battlegrounds. The first and most obvious is the assault from the secular society, pressuring us to compromise Christian principles and values. The second battleground is the pressure we face from people within the Church who do not hold to the values and principles of God's Word (as we will see later). The third battleground is the one we struggle with inside our minds. The battle is to gain control over the internal temptation to compromise. Since there are many fine books on the influence of secularism, the focus of this book will be on our own compromise, and that within the Church.

Examples of Moral Regression

Jeff and I worked together on the mission field. He was in his mid-thirties—articulate, multilingual and experienced. When he moved back to the States, he accepted a position as associate pastor and head of the singles ministry at a large church in Los Angeles. He was the protégé of a godly pastor and radio minister who had invested countless hours discipling him. One afternoon I received a call. To my astonishment, I learned that Jeff had become involved sexually with a woman in the singles group he was leading. *How could he be so foolish?* I wondered. *He knows better.*

Several weeks later, Jeff was in my office. I was bewildered to hear how neatly he catalogued his reasons for abandoning his wife and newborn daughter. "After all," he exclaimed, "divorce is not the unpardonable sin!" He had convinced himself that an adulterous relationship with a member of the church group he was leading was acceptable. As he left my office that day, my heart ached.

Jeff's story is by no means the first or the last. After a bored and lustful King David stole Uriah's wife, he tried in desperation to cover his sin. David ordered Joab, his chief of staff, to send Uriah to "the front line of the fiercest battle and withdraw from him" (2 Samuel 11:15, NASB). Uriah died and David took his wife as his own.

Some Christians use the moral failings of David or other Bible heroes to justify their own wrong choices. They reason, *If David, a man after God's own heart, could commit adultery and gain God's forgiveness, so can I.* Yet David suffered immensely for his sin. Scripture records the sad results. First, "The sword will never depart from your house" (2 Samuel 12:10). Second, "I will take your wives and give them to one who is close to you, and he will lie with your wives in broad daylight" (verse 11). Third, "The son born to you will die" (verse 14).

David did not cling to his sin or offer any excuse. He confessed and repented. Still, God did not remove the results of his bad choices. While God promises to forgive the contrite in heart, He does not promise to remove the painful effects of their choices.

King David serves as a positive example of how to deal with our sin. When we fail to respond properly, we head down the same tragic path as David's predecessor, King Saul (whom we will look at in chapter 3). The prophet Nathan confronted David with his sin and he repented. But when the prophet Samuel approached Saul with his, he excused it.

It is this excuse-making and rationalization of sinful behavior that have forged a new way of thinking in many of our churches. When excusing ourselves or blaming others for our sin becomes a habit, it leads to self-deception, which causes us to lose our capacity for clear moral reasoning. The moral potholes we have not dealt with in our lives prevent clear reasoning. With each act of self-will, our consciences begin to weaken. This in turn makes it harder to discern truth from error. When we rationalize our conduct, our lenses for viewing spiritual reality become scratched and dull, and we concoct our own rules. We may still believe everything is O.K.; yet the false notion that everything is fine, spiritually speaking, is one of the serious byproducts of self-deception. This can easily lead to an erroneous sense of God's favor on our lives or ministries.

Uncovering Deadly Obstacles

If we have engaged in self-deception and gotten off-track spiritually, how do we realign our lives? Since self-deception means lying to ourselves, it must, like any other sin, be removed. We know God desires truth in our inward parts (see Psalm 51:6), and that whenever the Bible refers to the heart, it is talking about the will. That is why Jesus said,

"The mouth speaks out of that which fills the heart" (Matthew 12:34, NASB). Our actions, opinions and attitudes flow from what is within our hearts. They become the expression of our wills. So the correct way to deal with any sin is first to recognize our vulnerability to sin, and then to acknowledge its presence in our lives.

Just acknowledging sin, however, is not enough. We must ask forgiveness of God and anyone we have hurt. Then we must repent or turn from our sin. Finally, if something is stolen or broken, we must make restitution, repairing or repaying what has been lost. If we are diligent to follow these scriptural guidelines, God will respond with forgiveness.

One purpose of this book is to expose the subtle ways you and I rationalize truth and compromise God's Word. When we recreate the meaning or significance of the Word, we reduce its absoluteness to our own moral level. Have you ever turned over a large rock to find bugs hiding underneath? When exposed to the light, these tiny creatures scurry for cover—and darkness. When we are exposed to the light of God's truth, it sends us scurrying. We either hide from God, as Adam and Eve did, or we fall on our knees and ask for God's cleansing and forgiveness. Let me assure you, turning over the stones in our lives is rarely a comfortable experience!

But while we must identify any self-deception in our own lives, this book will go beyond mere identification. It will also explain how self-deception takes root in a person's life. I hope, through the course of this book, that you will become more sensitized to the problem of self-deception in yourself and others. The process of identification is always the first step in mapping a remedy.

Here are some of the questions we will grapple with in the coming chapters:

- Why is recognizing absolute truth so important in furthering spiritual maturity?

- What happens when we engage in moral compromise?
- How is self-deception affecting the Body of Christ?
- What are the specific characteristics of those who are self-deceived?
- How can people act contrary to God's Word and still think they are doing His will?
- What is blasphemy against the Holy Spirit and how is it related to self-deception?
- What role does Satan play in self-deception?
- Is it possible for a person to see truth when he or she has been ignoring it for so long?
- What is our responsibility in confronting moral error within the Church?

Immoral or unethical behavior is one of the byproducts of self-deception, much the same as crime is one of the by-products of juvenile delinquency. It is often difficult, however, to pinpoint a single cause for either. Depending on who you talk to, for example, the causes of juvenile crime can be traced to one or more of the following factors: low socioeconomic status, parental abuse, a broken home, inadequate education, influence from television and movies, low self-esteem. Self-deception can follow a similar pattern. The causes can be traced to factors such as pride, compromise, excuse-making, disobedience to moral truth, distortion of Scripture and outright denial. We will look at each of these, in one form or another, in the first section of this book.

In chapter 2 let's begin to explore the subtle roots of self-deception in what I call "the mermaid syndrome."

Chapter Highlights

- Self-deception starts with rationalizing behavior we know is wrong.

- If making excuses or blaming others for our sin becomes a habit, it leads to self-deception. These "personal truths" become a form of self-preservation or a way to soothe our consciences.
- Self-deception is lying to ourselves about wrong choices. It can also be the passive acceptance of wrong choices in others.

Fighting
the Mermaid Syndrome

I don't steal. I don't lie. The way I look at it, I'm not sinning. He's not going to judge me. I don't think God judges anybody.

Geraldine Scott, prostitute

Self-centeredness may adopt a religious vocabulary and express itself in praiseworthy desires, but it remains self-centeredness.

Donald W. McCullough

A feeble, nominal Christianity is the greatest obstacle to the conversion of the world.

Henry Venn

The pastor of a community church in a small Northwestern town paid a visit to one of his parishioners. This was not just any member. It was the town's mayor. Three months before, the mayor had left his wife and children and moved in with the wife of the county assessor. Some members of the church were uncomfortable seeing the mayor sitting in church with the wife of the assessor. During a Sunday evening service led by the youth group, a teenager asked the congregation, "How can we expect to reach our community when we allow adultery in our own church?" Another church member later heard the mayor say, "If they kick me out of the church, I'll sue them for all they're worth." Perhaps because of pressure from a few godly elders, the pastor finally met with the mayor and his new companion, and reported later gleefully to the elders, "I really think they love each other!"

There are many who attend church and call themselves Christians who are like the mythical mermaid. They want the best part of two worlds—the benefits of Christianity without its injunctions to live a godly life. So, to solve their predicament, they try to live in both worlds.

When we minimize sinful behavior, as the mayor and pastor in this small town did, we encourage the mermaid syndrome. This thinking leads us to believe it is O.K. to break God's laws and still live in right standing with Him. But, partially through downplaying the seriousness of our wrong moral choices, the foundation of the American Church is being eaten away.

In 1832 Frenchman Alexis de Tocqueville observed, "A certain number of Americans pursue a peculiar form of worship from habit more than from conviction." De Tocqueville believed that two great dangers threatened Christianity in America: schism and indifference. Today we suffer from both. As we approach a new century, indifference to the demands of our faith is precisely what ails us. Let's look at several areas in which this indifference affects the Church:

- In a Janus Report on sexual behavior, the authors found that "very religious" people actually cheat on their spouses more than plain old religious people.[1]
- In a Northwestern University Medical School survey, researchers found that "adolescents who are good students and go to church are just as likely to

have sex as students who have divorced parents and low self-esteem."[2]

- Fifty-two percent of those who are born again, who go to conservative churches and who read the Bible say there is no such thing as truth.[3]
- A survey done by the Gallup organization found "dozens if not hundreds of young women on Christian college campuses every year quietly getting abortions. . . ."[4]
- Many "gender-neutral" seminaries and churches are trying to rewrite the Bible to fit their lifestyles or belief systems. For feminist theologians, according to a *Newsweek* article, "Patriarchy is the original sin and root of all other social evils: sexism, racism, clericalism, ageism, classism, homophobia, hatred of the body, parental subjugation of the children and mankind's technological rape of Mother Earth." These scholars are working feverishly to "strip the Bible of androcentric bias."[5]
- According to researcher George Barna, "Religion plays a surprisingly minor role in the entire divorce process." Barna noted that divorced Christians do not turn their backs on religion, but simply change churches and start all over again. He sums up the changing family landscape by saying, "No longer do traditional Christian values shape Americans' thinking."[6]

My underlying conviction is this: *Wrong thinking leads to wrong action*. As Christians we must not only know what God's Word says but be willing to do what it says. When we make choices we know are wrong, we are forced to develop a rationale for our choices, so that we can live, like mermaids, in two worlds at the same time.

In this chapter we will explore some of the reasons for the mermaid syndrome. Let's begin by examining the underlying cause of self-deceptive behavior. It is at the root of all moral compromise.

The Thorn in the Garden

It is paradoxical that one of Satan's names is *Lucifer*, which means "light-bearing" or "morning star." He poses as an angel of light, but in reality he is the prince of darkness. The prophet Ezekiel tells us the reason for Lucifer's fall:

> "You were internally filled with violence, and you sinned; therefore I have cast you as profane from the mountain of God. . . . Your heart was lifted up because of your beauty; you corrupted your wisdom by reason of your splendor."
> Ezekiel 28:16–17, NASB

Pride, what C. S. Lewis called "the great sin," led to Lucifer's expulsion from the presence of the Almighty. Don't be misled into thinking, *If I could just spend an hour in the presence of God, life would be different.* Satan remained in the presence of God, but it did not prevent him from thinking he could be like God.

Pride also led to man's exile from the Garden. In this setting Satan, disguised as a serpent, said to Eve, "God knows that when you eat of [the tree] your eyes will be opened, and you will be like God" (Genesis 3:5). God said, "The arrogance of your heart has deceived you" (Jeremiah 49:16 and Obadiah 1:3, NASB). Pride replaces God's rightful authority over our lives, separating us from Him.

Pride also leads to a suppression of truth. As we examine some of the subtle roots of self-deception, remember that the mantle of self-deception is often partial truth. In the Garden of Eden, the partial truth Satan presented was, "Your eyes will be opened." For the first time Eve saw what sin could do. But in response, after she and Adam had violated the only rule God had given them, they ran and hid in shame.

Our adversary uses partial truth to confuse and captivate his prey. We will see in the next chapter how this deception operated in the life of Saul, Israel's first king. Many cult leaders use partial truth to gain advantage over their followers. It works best on those most willing to compromise in some area of their lives. It also works well on those not well grounded in Scripture.

Lying to self and others, as well as the act of cloaking or covering our behavior, are common responses to sin. Adam and Eve did it. And until recently, most homosexuals also did it. In nearly every extramarital affair, there is some form of concealment. When God's Word says, "The truth will set you free" (John 8:32), it means that living an open and transparent life brings a deep sense of freedom. As youth evangelist and author Winkie Pratney says, "God did not design us for falsehood."

But those in deception harbor a growing fear that someone might find them out. As we will see later, this is one of the reasons a person in self-deception ignores correction. It is also one of the reasons we reject accountability.

While pride prevents further spiritual development, it does not stop the growth of knowledge. We often confuse one's knowledge of God's Word with obedience to it. True spiritual growth, however, comes from obeying the truth God reveals through His Word. As James tells us, "Do not merely listen to the word, and so deceive yourselves. Do what it says" (James 1:22).

Under certain circumstances, the Bible tells us, we are more susceptible to pride. Just when everything is going well for us, we are likely to forget God. In the tiny book of Hosea, God says, "As they had their pasture, they became satisfied, and being satisfied, their heart became proud; therefore, they forgot Me" (Hosea 13:6, NASB). The more God blessed His people, the more they turned their backs on Him. They no longer needed Him or saw Him as their provider. Today we do not have to trust God. We are self-sufficient; that is the American way. And the blessings He has graciously bestowed on us have become stumbling-blocks to our spiritual maturity.

Let's take a look at some other characteristics of pride:

- Poor listening ability (self-absorption causes discomfort in subordinate roles)
- Need to control others
- Lack of compassion for the plight of others (often, like the religious travelers in the story of the Good Samaritan, ignoring the most basic human needs)
- Masterful ability to flatter, peppering conversations with compliments designed to win others' approval
- Socially backward, rarely spending time with "ordinary" people
- Many superficial relationships but few, if any, intimate friendships
- Unwillingness to be truly accountable
- Unwillingness to receive constructive criticism

Whatever Became of Sin?

If pride is the mother of all sins—and the Bible makes it clear that it is—then why don't we hear more sermons about it? At least one reason may have to do with our disdain for dwelling on sin. Let's face it, sin is negative. It makes us feel bad. When was the last time you heard a message on sin and went away feeling good about yourself? Perhaps we think that by ignoring the negative aspects of sin, we can encourage good moral behavior in one another. I wish this worked, but it doesn't.

Judy, a missionary friend of ours, had a small cancerous growth on her face. For more than a year, my wife, Sue, and I begged her to have it examined by a doctor. She politely refused, until one day her son-in-law practically dragged her to a doctor. Fortunately the growth was cut out and no cancer was found. Ignoring the growth, however, had not made it go away.

Similarly, ignoring sin does not make it disappear. We cannot pretend serious issues into nonexistence. In psychological terms such attempts are called denial.

The difficulty many of us have with the concept of sin is that it nullifies everything the world teaches us to think about ourselves. It runs contrary to the notion of a positive self-image. It collides with those who believe in confessing only positive statements. In an article in *Atlantic Monthly,* author Glenn Tinder writes, "Nothing in Christian doctrine so offends people today as the stress on sin. It is morbid and self-destructive, supposedly to depreciate ourselves in this way." He concludes by observing, "Sin is ironic. Its intention is self-exaltation. Its result is self-debasement."[7]

True salvation implies a penitent heart. But penitent about what? Mistakes? Errors in judgment? Insensitivity? We are not exactly sure anymore. Repentance means turning away from sinful behavior. It means changing a lifestyle at odds with God's Word. Repentance keeps us in a state of humility before God and others. Many churchgoers are religious people who accept their sin rather than rely on the Holy Spirit to help them master it. Charles Colson calls this "the greatest paradox of our day." He writes: "Sin abounds in the midst of unprecedented religiosity. If there are so many of us, why are we not affecting our world?"[8]

One answer may be that our expectations are just too low. Or perhaps we are so inundated with "positive thinking" materials that there is little discussion about how to master sin. The actions of the mayor mentioned at the beginning of this chapter show that he is not interested in mastering sin. I am not sure he would even acknowledge that he is in sin. Nevertheless, one thing is clear. He is choosing to elevate his own will above God, the community he serves, his wife, family and fellow church members. When we receive Christ as Savior, we must also accept Him as our Lord and Master. If we accept Christ as Savior but ignore Him as Lord, we have not changed allegiances. We are still in bondage to self.

You see, what you and I think affects the way we behave. Thought always precedes action. If our thinking is misdirected due to errant teaching or false beliefs, our behavior will follow. We cannot accept the "convenient" theological tenets of the Gospel without the moral imperatives associated with His Lordship over our lives. The truth of the Gospel transforms people, and the empirical evidence of the power of the Gospel is found only in changed lives.

Nurturing the Supreme Virtue

We have noted that mermaid Christians want the best part of two distinct worlds—the benefits of Christianity without the inseparable injunctions to live a godly life. How do we throw off the mermaid syndrome? First, through nurturing the supreme virtue.

Jesus said to His disciples, "It is hard for a rich man to enter the kingdom of heaven. . . . It is easier for a camel to go through the eye of a needle than for a rich man to enter the kingdom of God" (Matthew 19:23–24). What did Jesus mean? The eye of the needle was a small door built into the larger city gate, a bit like a pet door for people. At dusk the people living inside the city closed the gate for their own protection. Any traveler who arrived after dusk was forced to sleep outside the city unless he could get through the "eye of the needle." A fully laden camel could squeeze through the small opening under certain arduous conditions. The burden it was carrying had to be taken off before the owner could lead the camel through on its knees. In a similar way, we must remove the obstacles that hinder us from entering the narrow gate.

Pride, which fosters an attitude of exclusivity, hinders our spiritual growth. It leads to spiritual blindness and neglecting others. Pride is what Jesus referred to when He said that the religious leaders of His day "outwardly appear righteous to men, but inwardly [they] are full of hypocrisy and lawlessness" (Matthew 23:28, NASB). They did their deeds "to be noticed by men" (verse 5, NASB). How could those who did everything by the rules be lawless? At least one reason was that they spent far more time protecting their images than doing the will of the Father.

The Prince of Peace would disappoint those who use the world's criteria to measure success. He who gave His life for us earned no university degree. He had no bank account. No retirement plan. He never owned a home. He frequently slept under the stars with no place to lay His head. He borrowed His transportation. He rarely knew where His next meal would come from. Yet He did not worry because He knew His heavenly Father would care for Him. His associates were criminals, minorities, outcasts and common laborers—the uncivilized and unrefined. There was nothing extraordinary about His upbringing or appearance. His value lay in internal beauty fashioned by the choices He made.

J. Oswald Sanders writes:

> If pride is the greatest and essential sin, then humility is the supreme virtue; and if humility was the distinguishing feature of the Master, then it must characterize the disciple.[9]

But for most of us, humility equals weakness. Who really strives to be humble? Rather, we steer conversations to center on us. We ignore the needs of others because our time is more important. These superficial indicators often tell us something about ourselves or others.

I am always amused when I find myself in conversation with other men I do not know well. Inevitably the first question is, "So, what do you do?" I always know what that means. It is my cue to provide the best verbal discourse I can on why I am a worthwhile human being. We males need to affirm ourselves through what we do. We derive a good part of our sense of identity from what others pay us to do for them. But this question is fueled by more than mere curiosity when the answer becomes the basis by which another person evaluates my worth.

Christ taught that the key to success was through the abasement rather than the glorification of self. He said, "Whoever exalts himself will be humbled, and whoever humbles himself will be exalted" (Matthew 23:12). And to His disciples He said, "Whoever wants to become great among you must be your servant" (Matthew 20:26). Today we have a veritable army of caring therapists adept at rebuilding self-esteem. Genuine self-esteem, however, is measured by its extrinsic manifestation of intrinsic values. The paradox of Christianity is that it undermines all that our culture considers of value. And a godly concept of self can come only from knowing the One who created us.

Embracing Confession

When the personal life and ministry of one evangelist came crashing to the ground, he handled it by encouraging his detractors to demonstrate "a spirit of love and reconciliation." He missed the point. His ministry, family and marriage were all in serious trouble. Yet he was directing his energy at controlling the damage his sinful behavior had created. As a result he lost his wife and his ministry.

When you find yourself facing a moral problem, what do you do? How do you deal with sin? Are you more concerned about people finding out? Do you wait until someone uncovers a skeleton in your closet? Or do you respond immediately to the pleading of the Holy Spirit?

I am always a bit suspicious when someone asks for forgiveness *after* he or she has been caught doing something wrong. It reminds me of a particularly humorous segment of "America's Funniest Home Videos." A four-year-old girl was caught on camera by her mother opening a drawer she was not supposed to get into. As soon as the startled little girl turned around, she said, "I love you, Mommy."

Self-deception can begin the moment we decide how to respond to our sin. Will we cover it up? Make excuses? Minimize its importance? Anytime we try to assuage guilt through making excuses, we become vulnerable to self-deception. This in turn weakens the Church by allowing behavior that is unacceptable. A sinful lifestyle thus becomes the incubator of self-deception. Author Gordon MacDonald explains:

> The Protestant penchant for privatizing faith and relegating confession to a singular transaction between that person and God has meant a loss of accountability. Anyone can breathe a silent prayer that amounts to little more than, "Sorry, God," and presume to get on with life. How, if things are to be so private and "under the table," is the sinner and the sinned against to know if there has been genuine sorrow and change of heart?[10]

Many of us have the misguided notion that no one has the right to interfere with our lives. We have become so private that nothing we do is anyone's business. When we accept Christ, however, we automatically become part of a community of believers. And part of our responsibility is getting involved in each other's lives.

I had a fleeting thought one day while pondering the breakup of yet another Christian marriage. *Why not gather together all the friends this couple knows*, I wondered, *and tell them we're not going to let them get a divorce? Instead of sitting back and saying, "Isn't it too bad Gene and Betty are getting a divorce?", what if we said, "We will do whatever we have to do to ensure that you get the help you need"?*

Godly intervention is what true Christian commitment is all about. (We will discuss a theology of confrontation in chapter 11.) But we trivialize confession because we do not really want to deal with the issues that make confession necessary. The idea of confession is much broader than simply saying, "I'm sorry." A forty-year-old Christian man I know had an affair with a woman he met at a gym. He confessed his sexual relationship to his wife and told her it was over. But now he was walking the long road back to spiritual and emotional restoration—a process that takes time, energy and commitment.

Confession is uncomfortable. It is hard work. As Gordon MacDonald points out, confession is more than simple recognition of sinful behavior. Acknowledging one's guilt is only the beginning step in the process of forgiveness. We must also add repentance and (where necessary) restitution. Whenever we try to circumvent or speed up God's prescription for wholeness, it interferes with the restorative process. So another way we can fight the mermaid syndrome is by dealing correctly and biblically with past transgressions instead of excusing or glossing over them.

My wife came home from shopping at a local thrift store one day. She had bought a wood headboard painted thickly in an ugly blue enamel. I wondered what had possibly motivated her to buy such an awful piece of furniture. I soon discovered the reason. On the reverse side of the headboard was stamped *Vermont maple.* Suddenly this ghastly headboard did not look so bad. During the next several months I spent many hours scraping the blue paint off that old headboard. Eventually the beautiful wood was bare and ready for refinishing. It was hard for me to understand why anyone would paint such beautiful wood. Why had they covered it up? The true value and beauty of the headboard became evident only after the old paint was removed.

Similarly, when we allow the Holy Spirit to strip bare what is in our hearts, the process of restoration can begin.

Understanding the Conditional Nature of Mercy

A proper understanding of one of the most misunderstood attributes of God's character, His mercy, can also help us fight the mermaid syndrome.

The Greek word for repent is *metanoeo,* meaning "to have a change of heart." The Hebrew derivative means "to return" or "to turn back." In either case *repent* is a proactive word. True repentance is not something God does; it is something we do. When we repent of our sin, it makes it possible for God to respond favorably to us and show mercy. God does not show mercy to those who are planning their next act of rebellion. He was willing to show mercy to the people of Nineveh because their hearts were moved by the warning Jonah brought them.

> When God saw what they did and how they turned from their evil ways, he had compassion and did not bring upon them the destruction he had threatened.
>
> Jonah 3:10

You might wonder what a discussion of God's mercy has to do with self-deception. How can mercy influence the weakening of the moral fiber of the Church?

Any researcher knows that the theoretical framework he uses will guide the very outcome of his work. A wrong framework produces distorted results. The same is true of biblical concepts like mercy. A distorted understanding of God's mercy makes transgressing His Word seem like "not such a big deal."

But God wanted to see the deeds of the people of Nineveh *before* He extended mercy to them. And He could not show mercy to them if they were planning secretly to rebel. We cannot use God's wonderful mercy as a way to cover over a conscience that can be cleared only by repentance. Otherwise it becomes easy to pass off the work of the Holy Spirit as needless condemnation. The person in self-deception uses the mercy of God as a shield to deflect criticism. He becomes untouchable and unaccountable and refuses to acknowledge the conditional nature of mercy.

The real issue is his unwillingness to change. He assumes that his behavior does not really matter to God.

Finding Grace to Do Right

We find within Christendom today a high regard for the grace of God. In fact, we so emphasize grace that we have neglected other divine attributes. God's grace, like His mercy, is misunderstood and misused. With this shield we deflect godly counsel, we divorce, we engage our senses in licentiousness and we refuse to come under godly pastoral leadership. In so doing we trample the miracle of God's grace.

The broad definition of *grace* that most of us use today is "God's unmerited favor." This definition of *grace* comes from the Old Testament, not the New. The Hebrew word *hen* refers to the favor that the strong bestow on the weak. A closely related verb is *hanan*, which means "to be gracious." In the New Testament the word is *charis*, whose verb form means to rejoice. It is the Old Testament definition that we most often apply to salvation, not the New.

Certainly the gift of Christ as the atoning sacrifice is the result of God's graciousness. We did nothing to deserve it. Salvation costs us no less today, however, than it did the first disciples: everything. Jesus said, "If anyone comes to me and does not hate his father and mother, his wife and children, his brothers and sisters—yes, even his own life—he cannot be my disciple" (Luke 14:26).

Jesus made no distinction between loving and obeying Him, and salvation itself. He said, "If anyone loves me, he will obey my teaching. My Father will love him, and we will come to him and make our home with him" (John 14:23). The plumb line that determines whether we know God is our obedience to Him. When we choose to disregard God's Word, we show little concern for what God thinks or expects of us.

> We know that we have come to know him if we obey his commands. The man who says, "I know him," but does not do what he commands is a liar, and the truth is not in him.
> 1 John 2:3–4

Author Zane Hodges is one of many Christians who reject the notion that salvation can be contingent upon anything, even obedience. This is tragic when you consider the numerous Scriptures attesting to the interrelationship between salvation and obedience. I am not suggesting, of course, that we attain salvation by our works. Rather, we confirm our salvation by our actions. But Hodges believes that regardless of how a person behaves, "Christ's absolutely free gift of salvation is possessed forever." He continues, "To include faith in repentance is repugnant."[11]

If ever there were an excuse to live like a spiritual mermaid, this sloppy theology would make it easy! This interpretation gives pseudo-spiritual license to those who believe they can attain salvation by repeating a few phrases. Such "force-fit" salvations usually amount to little more than an unending cycle of moral wreckage. When we declare the most unpenitent sinner born again, we pollute the work of the cross, giving birth to hypocrisy and fanning the flames of secular malevolence.

The confusion wrought by such books does not have its origin in the Bible. It comes, sad to say, from a handful of early reformers like Martin Luther. Luther taught that sin is an inevitable and acceptable part of the Christian's life:

> Sin boldly, but believe and rejoice in Christ more boldly still. You are a sinner anyway and there is nothing you can do about it. You are a sinner so be a sinner and don't try to become what you are not. Yes, become a sinner again and again every day.[12]

Contrast Luther's statement with the apostle Paul: "Do not let sin reign in your mortal body so that you obey its evil desires" (Romans 6:12).

Suppose a young man proposes to his girlfriend. She accepts his invitation excitedly. Soon they begin making plans for their wedding. Then, as the day draws near, the young man tells his fiancée about his mistress. "Please be patient with me," he tells her. "Within a year I'll break off that relationship. I just need time." She responds by saying, "Let me know when you make up your mind. Then we can talk about marriage!" The young woman reasons that if the young man loves her, he will be willing to give up the other woman.

Most of us would not think of continuing a relationship on such a basis. But we, like the young man, expect God to ignore the areas of our lives that hinder the consummation of our relationship with Him. Contemporary teaching—that Christians sin every day in thought, word and deed—mirrors this misleading concept. We accept a defeatist mentality toward sin while extolling the virtues of positive thinking.

To be sure, we must not use God's Word to pound one another into compliance. But neither must we use His grace to excuse us from obeying Him. Our goal is to rely on God's grace to live as we should, rather than use it as a license to do as we please. If we employ God's grace as a pretext to reduce the seriousness of sin, we lose sight of how immoral choices separate us from our Creator. And to treat sin as Hodges or Luther did is a blatant contradiction of God's redeeming power to free us from the strength of sin.

Once again I emphasize that *wrong thinking leads to wrong action.* As Christians we must know what God's Word says and be willing to obey, so that we do not make choices we know are wrong, and then have to develop a rationale for those choices. Doing so (as we will see in the next chapter) is a process that leads to self-deception.

In Eve's case, self-deception began when she confused what looked *good* with what was *right.* When we focus exclusively on what looks good, we assume it must be from God and are blinded to what He wants for us. Whatever produces (or whatever we perceive to produce) a "bad" result is wrong. But according to this logic, our quest for a more comfortable lifestyle could lead to a questionable business deal, since we assume the "good" end must be God's blessing. In this distortion of truth, we see choices as wrong only if their desired ends are unacceptable to us.

Self-deception usually begins with small things or simple instructions, but it leads to serious results—even death.

Chapter Highlights

- Wrong thinking leads to wrong action.
- The root of all self-deception is pride. Pride is a way of elevating our own wills above God's.
- When we sin, our response must include the following elements: acknowledgment, confession, repentance and (where needed) restitution. Simply acknowledging our sin stops short of allowing God to work in our hearts.

- The mercy of God is contingent upon our willingness to turn from our sin. Repentance is the attitude of heart that enables God to forgive us and show His mercy.
- The grace of God is not license to do as we please but should motivate us to live as we should. An overemphasis on any single divine attribute can lead to a warped understanding of God.

Having It Our Way

The right act is simply the one that yields the agent the most exciting challenge or the most good feeling about himself . . . Bending the rules makes sense if it enhances the player's satisfaction.

> Robert Bellah

Jesus never said, "If you want to be My disciple go out and fulfill yourself." He said, "Take up your cross, deny yourself and follow Me."

> Sister Bernadette Counihan

A commercial for fast food giant Burger King used a catchy song to sell hamburgers several years ago: "Have it your way. . . ." It soon came to symbolize the American way, in which choice is one of the virtues we esteem the most.

This point was hammered home to me when I lived in northern Israel. The local market carried just two kinds of cereal—cornflakes and Rice Krispies. Whenever Sue and I made the three-hour drive to Tel Aviv, we always took time to stop by a more American-style grocery store that carried a dozen varieties of cereal. Patrons were glad to pay three times the U.S. price for the privilege of having a choice.

We bring the idea of choice into every compartment of our lives. We demand options in our hamburgers, our children's education and our churches. We even want a choice about how we live or die. But when we grow up believing that choice is synonymous with rightness, it is easy to slip into applying this false theology to our moral and spiritual lives.

Peter Gomes is Harvard's Plummer Professor of Christian Morals. Gomes is also gay. It comes as no surprise that he rejects biblical interpretations condemning his homosexual practice. "Those who use the Bible to denigrate homosexuals," he says, "have taken the book's words out of its historical context. The biblical writers never contemplated a form of homosexuality in which loving and faithful persons sought to live out the implications of the Gospel with as much fidelity to it as any heterosexual believer."[1]

For Gomes, personal lifestyle and behavior serve as the guide on moral issues. In other words, he wants to have it his way. That is precisely the difficulty many Christians now face. Do we stick to the absoluteness of God's ways or create our own morality based on what we perceive as best for us?

Some observers have a growing sense that American culture is on a terrific revision downward. Columnist George Will calls ours "a trickle-down culture."[2] The problem is that what is trickling down from the top is not self-sacrifice or moral values; it is the drive to satisfy every impulse. *U.S. News & World Report* columnist John Leo believes we have destigmatized sexual behavior to such a degree that divorce has become society's accepted ailment.[3] The fact is, to package moral bondage as attractively as possible is part of Satan's plan.

Joseph Califano, a former U.S. Secretary of Health, Education and Welfare, underscores our moral decline. He deplores our "anything-goes moral standards, the declining authority of the family, church and school, and a mass culture that treats sex not as a serious personal responsibility [but] as a glittering consumer item to be exploited and consumed at the moment of desire."[4] Even television writer and producer Norman Lear observes that "short-term thinking, corrosive individualism, fixating on 'economic man' at the expense of the human spirit, has taken an alarming role."[5]

The so-called value-free decision-making that became popular in the late 1960s has left moral carnage that will take years to clean up. William Kilpatrick, professor of education at Boston College, says we have become "morally polluted." Teachers are already supplanting parents, Kilpatrick believes, by teaching a moral of non-morality. In our quest to avoid moral indoctrination, we have left a vacuum that can be filled only by moral absolutes.[6]

This so-called value-free environment is supposed to produce a more culturally enlightened student devoid of the handicaps engendered by Christian zealots. Unfortunately, many of today's cultural surveyors are not voices emanating from the pulpit. They are educators, journalists and entertainment executives who recognize the need for some kind of moral reentrenchment.

Although Americans believe that having options is important to their lives, biblical morality does not work like this. The mark of a believer is not insisting on his own way, but rather allowing God to have His way. This is where we often run into trouble. An emphasis on individual rights easily becomes a self-centered effort to control our surroundings. Our desire to have things our way can lead to blame-shifting and eventually to compromise in small or larger areas.

Spreading the Blame

I attended a political meeting one evening in which the director of our county public works department shared the speaking duties. Byron, a 52-year-old public servant, told us a harrowing story. He and his wife were driving home one evening in California following a dinner engagement when a car careened around a dark curve on the highway. Although he tried to avoid a collision, Byron was helpless. It was as if the driver was aiming right for him. After the powerful impact sent shrapnel and glass scattering everywhere, Byron's wife lay dead. He was rushed to a nearby hospital in critical condition.

The driver of the car that hit Byron and killed his wife was drunk. He survived the accident and immediately posted bail. It was his third arrest for drunk driving. He promptly filed a lawsuit against the state of California for failing to place better signs along the highway. Byron was also named in the lawsuit. The drunk driver won his case and collected $250,000.

It is a fact well lamented that we not only have it our way, but we excuse our behavior, then take it a step further by blaming the victim. America has earned a reputation as one of the most litigious nations in the world. As Byron's story illustrates, we are prone to blaming others for every bad experience. The advocates of individual rights have fostered a growing sense of entitlement, stretching from single mothers on welfare to multimillion-dollar professional athletes. The Church is far from immune to this "social disease."

To the extent that we believe we deserve something, it becomes easier for us to justify questionable means of attaining it. Think, for example, how easy it is to go into debt to get something we really "need," or to break a promise to spouse or children because a "better" opportunity presented itself.

The problem, according to journalist Phil Rosenthal,

is that no one takes responsibility for their own actions anymore. It's always someone else's fault. No one is held accountable anymore. We are losing our moral bearings. . . .

People say they cannot tell right from wrong, and we accept that.[7]

From the earliest days in Eden, humans have looked outside themselves to place blame. There are special groups for every imaginable problem—alcohol, drugs, sex addiction, gambling, eating and shopping. We affix the *disease* label to many of these difficulties. But in many respects this is just another way to transfer personal responsibility. And we genuinely believe what we are told by the professionals: "Whatever you've done, it's really not your fault." The blame gets shifted to the external environment—a bad home life, low self-esteem, stress or a genetic predisposition.

Social pundit Scott Montgomery writes:

> We jettison morality because we think happiness is more important. . . . Psychoanalysis, aided by clinical studies that suggest links between behavior and biology, has reinforced notions that we are not responsible for ourselves. We are guided by genetics, not choices.[8]

The late psychiatrist Karl Menninger wrote in *Whatever Became of Sin?*:

> Notions of guilt and sin which formerly served as some restraint on aggression have become eroded by the presumption that the individual has less to do with his actions than we assumed, and hence any sense of personal responsibility (or guilt) is inappropriate. This philosophy comes as a comforting relief for many.[9]

If our bad behavior is motivated by sickness, disease or poor upbringing, we are surely not responsible for it. Again, the Bible teaches us not about moral illness but about rebellion. This flows from a heart bent on having things its own way. And, as we can see in the life of Israel's first king, there is a very real connection between refusing to take responsibility for our actions and self-deception.

King Saul: A Case Study in Self-Will

For four hundred years the tribes of Israel were ruled by a succession of leaders called judges—temporary saviors God raised up when His people were in trouble. God had been their protector, provider, guide and judge ever since He called them out of the land of Egypt. But the people wanted to "be like all the other nations" (1 Samuel 8:20). They wanted a king. Although it was not part of God's original plan, He gave in to the demands of the Israelites. Sadly, their desire to be like other nations was their initial step toward rejecting God's rulership over their lives (see 1 Samuel 8:7). They wanted their own way.

God made sure the Israelites—through Samuel, Israel's last judge—knew the consequences of their choice. To be like the other nations, they would face military conscription, then forced labor to meet the needs of the king and his household. Finally, warned Samuel, when the people cried out because of their king, "The LORD will not answer you in that day" (1 Samuel 8:18). But the Bible tells us that "the people refused to listen" (verse 19).

Many wonder why God is silent in their lives. He may be permitting us, as He did the people of Israel, to have what we want, but there are always consequences associated with our decisions. God's Word says, "He gave them their request; but sent leanness into their soul" (Psalm 106:15, KJV).

In response to the Israelites, God selected the finest physical specimen among all the tribes. His name was Saul. God tested Saul, as He did those who followed in his footsteps. Would Saul obey God's commands? Would he be willing to submit his will to God's?

Warning Signs

The first test Saul faced was trust. Samuel, the spiritual authority of the Israelites, instructed Saul to wait for him for seven days in Gilgal, where Samuel would offer sacrifices (see 1 Samuel 10:8). But the Philistines were gathering for battle and Saul's troops were frightened. Saul did not trust God completely. "He waited seven days, the time set by Samuel; but Samuel did not come . . . and Saul's men began to scatter" (1 Samuel 13:8). He wanted to get on with "God's business." So Saul rushed ahead on his own, reasoning that with the troops scattering, he had to maintain control. After all, isn't that what leadership is all about?

Saul moved ahead of God, for reasons that sounded good, and made the necessary sacrifices himself. In so doing, he put himself, the political-military leader, in the role of spiritual leader—a position God never intended.

There are always warning signs in our lives when something is morally askew. Saul's impatience was evidence of his lack of trust in God. His unwillingness to wait and his propensity to be controlled by the urgency of the situation led him to take matters into his own hands. He made one of the classic mistakes we make today. He assumed that God's will is always dynamic, and he associated action with rightness because he was the anointed king. But in his haste he was presumptuous. (When we rush ahead of God's timing, we, too, are tempted to justify our choices, sometimes using a very spiritual-sounding rationale.)

When Samuel finally arrived, he asked Saul about the premature sacrifices. Here is how Saul should have responded: "I have sinned. I am guilty. Please forgive me." Instead he sought to justify his wrong choices, saying, "I forced myself and offered the burnt offering" (1 Samuel 13:12, NASB). The moment he refused to acknowledge his own guilt, he was in self-deception. This made it necessary for him to find a suitable explanation that would pacify his conscience.

Despite Saul's sin, the Lord sent panic on the Philistines and "rescued Israel that day" (1 Samuel 14:23). Even so, Samuel told Saul that "you acted foolishly" (1 Samuel 13:13) and "now your kingdom will not endure" (verse 14).

Into the Quicksand

The second test Saul faced was obedience, when Samuel issued another command of God to the king: "Go, attack the Amalekites and totally destroy everything that belongs to them. Do not spare them; put to death [everyone and everything]" (1 Samuel 15:3). God places less value on material things than we do. He was not concerned about the loss of life or animals for possible sacrifice. He was interested in just one thing: How would Saul respond to His word?

Once again Saul did not obey the command. He spared Agag, king of Amalek, and the best of the sheep, oxen, lambs and "everything that was good" (verse 9).

By today's standards, what Saul did makes sense. He spared the best. But those of us who cling to the world's value system will never understand God's. Obedience is not an economic matter; it is a spiritual one. And our virtue lies not in the quantity of what we accumulate, but in the quality of our moral choices. As in Saul's case, an overemphasis on material things can easily get in the way of our obeying God.

The fascinating thing about the ensuing battle is that once again the Israelites won. From the perspective of his troops, Saul was a hero. And the young king drew a terrible conclusion from this victory. He thought God was concerned only with the outcome. In reality, in Saul's selective obedience, he had set his will against God's. And when the battle was over, Saul "set up a monument in his own honor" (1 Samuel 15:12).

Saul's self-exaltation blinded him to the seriousness of his disobedience. He was losing touch with spiritual reality. Saul chose to glorify himself instead of God. The intoxicating effect of pride is that it limits our ability to see ourselves as God or others see us. When we allow pride in our lives, it clogs our spiritual arteries. This stops the life-sustaining flow that helps us communicate with God. When we allow pride in our lives, we soon lose touch with Him. God says that even if "you spread out your hands in prayer, I will hide My eyes from you, yes, even though you multiply prayers, I will not listen" (Isaiah 1:15, NASB).

Saul decided to override God's explicit word so he could have things his way. This was a tragic decision, the next step in a process that led Saul into self-deception. Saul's actions did not dictate against his will; they rose out of it. His choices, like yours and mine, determined what his moral character would be. It is overly simplistic to see Saul as just another sinner. He was that. But this explains nothing and leads us nowhere. Saul was a sinner because he chose to rebel. Although he understood the command of the Lord, he was unwilling to carry it out completely, preferring his own will over God's.

The first thing Saul did was take matters into his own hands. Then he set his will above God's. Finally he failed to take responsibility for his disobedience.

God gave Saul another chance to repent by sending His messenger Samuel. But before God's prophet could speak a word, the king said, "I have carried out the LORD's instructions" (1 Samuel 15:13). Pride had blinded Saul to the seriousness of what he had done, destroying only what was worthless among the Amalekites, rather than everything, as God had commanded. He was looking only at the end result of the victorious battle.

Samuel bought none of it. He said, "What then is this bleating of sheep in my ears?" (verse 14).

Saul's reply indicates how he tried to spread the blame, just as Eve blamed the serpent and Adam blamed Eve. Saul said, "The soldiers . . . spared the best of the sheep and cattle to sacrifice to the LORD your God" (verse 15). From this point on, Saul began to lose touch with spiritual reality. Notice his reference to "your God" rather than "my God." He came to the realization that God was far from him.

It would have been easier for Samuel to say, "You did a pretty good job, Saul. After all, this was your first time around, and God understands nobody's perfect." In many of our churches, we would opt for a more "balanced" approach—more loving and merciful. In fact, some of us might even see Samuel as divisive, critical or judgmental. But, like a trial lawyer, Samuel continued to press the issue of Saul's rebellion. He restated God's call, command and mission for the king. Again Saul insisted he had obeyed the voice of the Lord, and repeated his reason for keeping the spoils: "to sacrifice them to the LORD your God" (verse 21).

Samuel could have responded, "I understand the dilemma you were in. Since you were really doing it for God, I'm sure He understands." But this is not what Samuel said. He gave his classic response in the form of a question:

> "Has the Lord as much delight in burnt offerings and sacrifices as in obeying the voice of the Lord? To obey is better than sacrifice . . . rebellion is as the sin of divination and insubordination is as iniquity and idolatry."
>
> 1 Samuel 15:22, NASB

The connection between divination and rebellion is a curious one. Divination is a method of discovering the future in order to determine the divine will. But divination and rebellion both circumvent God's path. They displace God in their quest for knowledge. They are both ways of saying, "I want what I want and I want it now." But God wants our trust, our dependence. He wants us to be patient, for it is through patience that He develops character and trust in us.

Your Way or God's Way?

It had been perfectly clear to Saul what God's orders were, just as the Israelites had understood God's warnings about a king. And it is the same with us today. Our difficulty is not in understanding what God is saying to us. Our problem is doing what He says.

Self-deception begins when, through pride, we elevate our will above God's. This leads to making excuses for immoral choices. God says, "The man who says, 'I know him,' but does not do what he commands is a liar, and the truth is not in him" (1 John 2:4). Before Saul began to reign, God warned the Israelites to "fear the LORD and serve Him in truth with all your heart" (1 Samuel 12:24, NASB). But Saul failed to guard truth as something precious.

Saul finally acknowledged that he had sinned. But this did not occur until after God rejected him from being king. Saul also revealed to Samuel his true motive for his sin:

> "I was afraid of the people and so I gave in to them. Now I beg you, forgive my sin. . . . But please honor me before the elders of my people and before Israel; come back with me. . . ."
>
> 1 Samuel 15:24–25, 30

Saul knew that Samuel revered God and that the people respected Samuel. If Samuel failed to return with Saul, the people might start wondering about their king. So, in desperation, Saul tore Samuel's robe, begging him to return with him. Saul valued the approval of others above the approval of God. After this sad incident, the Bible says,

"Samuel did not see Saul again until the day of his death" (verse 35, NASB).

The final tragedy of rebellion is that it separates us from God and from one another. When we choose our own way, someone else inevitably suffers. Since having our way requires putting ourselves first, others must live with whatever choices we make. We can see this pattern in parents whose pursuit of personal fulfillment leaves their children hurt, angry or disillusioned. A father who abandons his family sets his wife and children up for poverty and lower educational attainment. And fatherless homes add dramatically to the crime rate and welfare rolls.

God loved Saul. God sought restoration. He gave Saul several chances to acknowledge and repent of his disobedience. Yet Saul rejected God.

How you and I deal with sin in our lives determines our susceptibility to self-deception. God, in His wisdom, rarely takes us beyond our last step of obedience. And if we make excuses for partial obedience, we may wind up as Saul did—cut off from God.

In the next chapter we will explore some of the ways our society has rejected objective truth. The impact of secularization on the Church affects the way we view absolute truth. Our secular heritage has left us destitute and directionless in the moral arena. And while nearly everyone is recognizing the need to reintroduce moral teaching, no one is quite sure how to implement it.

Chapter Highlights

- Do you excuse wrong behavior in your life or the lives of others? If so, why?
- Are you impatient? Do you move ahead on important decisions before you know what God wants you to do?

- Be on guard for these early warning signs of self-deception:

  Do you blame others for your own wrong choices?

  Do you try to control circumstances or people?

  Do you place a high value on material things?

  Do you care more about what others think about you than in doing what is right?

  Do you view progress or success as verification that you have done the right thing?

Excuses: Betraying the Truth

If everybody's doing it, then why shouldn't I? This rationalization has begun to take hold in all areas of our lives. Once woven into the fabric of our beliefs, it is where our most serious troubles begin. We no longer can tell right from wrong.

The Day America Told the Truth

The test of first-rate intelligence is the ability to hold two opposing ideas in the mind and still retain the ability to function.

F. Scott Fitzgerald

The insurance company told a Miami woman that it would pay to fix the damages to her roof after a hurricane swept through the area. Then it accidentally sent her a check to have the entire roof replaced. "I know it's wrong," she said, "but I'm keeping it anyway. I've paid premiums since I was eighteen years old and I've never claimed anything before."[1]

At the root of any moral breakdown is a willingness on the part of ordinary people to compromise morality. Eventually they are no longer able to think objectively about what constitutes right and wrong. God declares, "Woe to those who call evil good and good evil" (Isaiah 5:20). But we raise a more practical question: "What's best for me?"

The story of Amy Grossberg and Brian Peterson Jr. illustrates this. Grossberg, a college freshman, was in labor when she called Peterson, her boyfriend, late one evening in November 1996. The two eighteen-year-olds decided to rendezvous at a Comfort Inn in Newark, Delaware, where "Baby Grossberg" was born at four A.M. Peterson reportedly wrapped the six-pound-two-ounce newborn in a garbage bag and threw it into a trash dumpster. The autopsy revealed that the baby died from multiple skull fractures with injury to the brain "due to blunt force head trauma and shaking." According to his attorney, Peterson expressed no sorrow over the death of the child. "No one knows what to think," said Brian Thalman, a high school friend.[2]

Peterson and Grossberg were not hardened criminals with a history of misconduct. They were a couple of "nice kids" from affluent families. They were happy, successful, well-liked. So why did they do it? The answer is not so simple. Perhaps they did not want the baby to ruin their college plans. Or maybe they wanted to avoid the stigma of out-of-wedlock parenthood. Whatever the answer, the crime shocked nearly everyone who heard about it. *Time* columnist Margaret Carlson reflected, "Perhaps [Peterson's] conscience has been warped somewhere along the way."[3]

She is right, of course. But should we be surprised? Why would two young people *not* be tempted to take the life of their newborn, when to abort a baby before birth is an acceptable alternative these days and when we are taught to think primarily of ourselves?

But morality is not simply a roadblock on the path to self-preservation or pleasure. And the troubling of the conscience is intended to encourage us to make things right with our Creator. God has designed us to listen to our consciences and avoid sin, or to return, after we do sin, to a right relationship with Him. (We will look at the function of the conscience in the next chapter.) But although God's purpose is always to restore, we can expect the great deceiver to do all he can to interrupt this process. If he can get us to view immoral behavior as justifiable in some way or inevitable or even acceptable, he will succeed in keeping us in bondage. (We will see in chapter 8 how Satan works to pervert truth.)

We begin, Christians and non-Christians alike, by making excuses.

The Mechanics of Excuse-Making

Anyone who has ever lived with small children knows what rationalization is all about. Children are skillful at deflecting responsibility for broken windows, missing cookies or misplaced homework. These excuses make parenting tough work. Yet even as adults we have a tendency to blame others when we are caught doing something we should not. And self-deception begins when we manufacture excuses. Excuse-making is a way of placing blame somewhere else.

In the beginning excuses are conscious choices designed to protect us from rejection, embarrassment or discomfort. Ultimately they are a way of refusing to take personal responsibility.

Let's look at seven areas in which our society has made serious compromise. (These are just the tip of the iceberg!) Both the behavior and the excuses for the behavior are designed to make immoral choices appear morally acceptable.

1. Tolerating Immorality

According to a poll conducted by the Josephson Institute of Ethics, 24 percent of high school students agreed with this statement: "It is not unethical to do whatever you have to do to succeed if you don't seriously hurt other people."[4]

Lisa Schiffren became famous for writing former Vice President Dan Quayle's speech castigating the TV character Murphy Brown for bearing a child out of wedlock. But in an interview about sexuality, Schiffren said, "I did not abstain from premarital sex. I was raised in a secular, Upper East Side Manhattan–liberal home, and now I'm a quasi-religious conservative. I wish I could say that premarital sex was wrong. Sometimes I think it's O.K. We really don't want people getting married too, too early."[5] Schiffren's excuses for her own sexual experimentation range from blaming her secular background to society's attitudes toward abstinence.

In the New York City school system, educators locked horns with parents about how to teach sexual tolerance to young students. One report called on first-grade teachers to "include references to lesbian/gay people in all curricular areas." The suggested reading list for these impressionable young minds included *Heather Has Two Mommies* and *Daddy's Roommate*, which includes an illustration of two men in bed.[6] The following quote from a book titled *Gloria Goes to Gay Pride* is designed to help children ages three to seven become more tolerant of homosexuals: "Some women love women, some men love men. Some women and men love each other. That's why we march in the parade—so everyone can have a choice."[7] While prayer in public schools is still hotly debated, our value-free education teaches tolerance for immorality.

The problem is not limited to young people. The entertainment industry offers all of us a steady diet of sex, violence and profanity. Although it collects billions of dollars in advertising revenue, it refuses to acknowledge the social impact of its menu. According to film critic Bob Strauss, it is getting impossible to establish a national moral consensus. "Without generally accepted guidelines to live by," he asks, "can widespread moral apathy be far behind?" Many films in the 1990s, he observes, "attach their audiences' sympathies to characters who cut corners to achieve their goals."[8]

It comes as no surprise that excuses for poor moral choices are made by those in political life, too. Newt Gingrich launched his first congressional campaign in Georgia on a "return to moral values." A few years later he shed his first wife, who had been his high school math teacher. While Mrs. Gingrich lay in a hospital bed recovering from cancer surgery, he showed up with a yellow legal pad to discuss the terms of their divorce. When Gingrich was quizzed about this later, he offered the following excuse: "When you marry your high school math teacher and grow in different directions, there is an evolutionary process."[9]

2. Relabeling Sin

Several years ago I spoke in a church in a small north Idaho town. After the service I joined several people in the congregation for a boat ride on Lake Pend Orielle. John, a well-to-do, middle-aged realtor, told me how drinking had nearly destroyed his life. Countless times, he said, he had felt drawn to a nearby bar as if beckoned by the sirens of alcohol. Like the sailors in Greek mythology lured by sea nymphs to their deaths on the rugged Adriatic coast, John had lost control.

After he poured out his sad story to me, I mustered the courage to ask him the inevitable question: "Why do you keep drinking?"

"Oh, I can't help it," John replied matter-of-factly. "It's a disease."

I dared to probe further. "If alcoholism is a disease, why do you feel bad about it?"

"Because I know it's wrong."

"But if you can't help yourself, then God wouldn't hold you responsible, would He?"

Now John was confused. He seemed convinced that because of a possible genetic predisposition to alcoholism, he could not therefore assume responsibility and stop drinking.

His attitude did not help him deal with his problem; it only convinced him to duck responsibility. He was in bondage to alcohol, and his excuse had become the stumblingblock to his recovery.

The best that can be said about research on the genetics of alcoholism, according to a recent report in *U.S. News & World Report,* is that it is inconclusive. An article titled "Politics and Biology" asserts: "The issues of choice and responsibility come up again and again in the discussion of alcoholism and other addictive disorders. Many are concerned about the widely accepted disease model of alcoholism that actually provides people with an excuse for their destructive behavior."[10]

Psychiatrist William Glasser, in his classic work *Reality Therapy,* commented: "People do not act irresponsibly because they are 'ill'; they are 'ill' because they act irresponsibly."[11] There are many different reasons people want to escape reality, including financial struggles, loneliness, job stress, marital unhappiness, the death of a loved one. Whatever the cause, many today believe that the process of labeling bad or sick behavior serves to perpetuate it. Many labels are unacceptable, too stigmatizing—so we change them. The delinquent youth is not a criminal; he is *maladjusted.* The woman who beats her children suffers from *coping problems.* And the alcoholic is simply *dysfunctional.*

These labels serve their purpose by erasing—or at least easing—the stigma associated with the behavior. But the new terms fail to do anything to change irresponsible or immoral behavior.

I was in a Christian bookstore in Los Angeles surveying the inventory of self-help books. I found more than thirty titles on inner healing, self-improvement and self-esteem. I found one title on humility. On my way out I shared my frustration with the clerk, who replied apologetically, "If I'm honest, Jesus just doesn't meet the needs of many Christians today."

Is it true that the flourishing market for self-help books shows our lack of confidence in the completeness of Christ? Is Jesus unable to meet our need for emotional or mental healing? Is His teaching too simplistic for our technological age? If His words are not the answer, where else can we turn? There are many fine programs to strengthen marriages, provide coping skills and reduce stress. But shifting our reliance from Christ to techniques rarely addresses some of the root problems affecting our emotional well-being: our own sin and sins committed against us.

In his book *Sin, the Ultimate Deadly Addiction,* J. Keith Miller observes that substance abuse and codependency can be a way we shelter ourselves from personal responsibility. Sin, he says, is "a blinding self-absorption, the universal self that develops when individuals put themselves in the center of their personal world in a way that leads to abuse of others and self."[12]

Mental illness, childhood trauma, alcoholism and emotional abuse are just a few of the excuses we accept today. One national magazine observes: "Blaming parents for what they did or didn't do has become a national obsession. In the adult children [of alcoholics] movement there may be little talk of forgiveness, much about blame."[13] Those who are genuine victims need our compassion and care. Nevertheless, their victimization is not a cause of their later sinful behavior. As painful as our life experiences have been, they are no excuse for walking contrary to God's ways. The moment we accept excuses for sinful conduct, we remove personal responsibility.

3. Sodom's Children

Former talk show host Phil Donahue was quizzing a panel of homosexual actors who made pornographic films. With so many people dying of AIDS, he asked, how could they justify their performances? One man explained, "I view what I'm doing as educational. It teaches other men how to have safe sex."

Beyond excusing immorality, there is blaming others for it. The Reverend Troy Perry, founder of the gay Metropolitan Community Church, advises his parishioners, "You don't owe apologies to anybody. Don't let those idiotically bigoted Christian groups in this country . . . tell you you can't be spiritual."[14] The Reverend Peter Gomes, the homosexual professor I mentioned in the last chapter, blames the Church for forcing homosexuality "into patterns that are not healthy or productive."[15]

The causes of homosexuality are debated hotly inside and outside the Church. Many believe in genetic causation. There is a monumental difference, of course, between causation and predisposition. But there is no solid research showing that people are born homosexual. A well-publicized study in 1991 by Simon LeVay (a homosexual) found a certain nucleus in the hypothalamus that was more than twice the size in gay men as in heterosexual men. He was unable to demonstrate, however, how this made a difference. Another study in 1993 by Dean Hamer identified a genetic marker on the X chromosome in 75 percent of homosexual men. Additional research has not been successful in replicating Hamer's results.

A growing number of studies have tried to find a link between certain human behavior and genetics. The question most Christians need to answer is, To what extent, if any, is our behavior determined by forces beyond our control? The aggressive shift to neurogenetic determinism as an explanation for human behavior can serve as a convenient excuse and enable us to betray the truth about our own choices and responsibility. But as we look to the Bible, we see no underlying excuses offered to the men of Sodom, the woman at the well who had five husbands, or the woman caught in adultery. Genetics was not an issue; obedience was.

This is not to say that a son raised by an overbearing and controlling mother, and a daughter whose father molested her sexually, are not affected by the sinful choices of others and cannot be influenced toward homosexual behavior. But if the residents of Sodom suffered from a genetic predisposition toward homosexuality, why did God destroy them? Would this not have been an unjust act by a just and merciful Creator?

And why was sexual perversion so rampant in this one place? Homosexuals today claim that the sin of Sodom was inhospitality. But the men of Sodom demanding that Lot allow them to have sex with his angelic guests (see Genesis 19:4–5) can hardly be construed as a lack of hospitality. God's Word says that "Sodom and . . . the surrounding towns gave themselves up to sexual immorality and perversion" (Jude 7). The men of Sodom were so consumed with lust that they could no longer reason or act with any moral clarity.

4. Conjugal Treason

In 1997 the Presbyterian Church (U.S.A.) passed the Fidelity and Chastity Amendment requiring celibacy of all unmarried ministers, deacons and elders. But some protesting leaders, like the Reverend Robert Craig, pastor of the historic New York Avenue Presbyterian Church in Washington, D.C., offered a unique reason for his outrage at the new church law. "It's tough enough, being a downtown urban church, to attract people, in particular young adults," he complained. "But this action has done damage to the name *Presbyterian* to the point where our process of evangelization and outreach has been impeded."[16]

A woman wrote to Ann Landers about her troubled marriage: "My husband and I have been married for twenty-five years. We are both Christians and active in our church. Last year I discovered that I had genital herpes. I was in a state of shock. My husband has said, time and time again, 'I have not been with anyone else.' I feel as if I'm living with a man I don't know anymore."

Sad to say, this is not an isolated case. A Roper survey found that 25 percent of born-again Christians had had an extramarital affair *after* their conversion experience.[17] This appalling statistic should cause the Church to examine what it is teaching. How many times have you heard one of the following comments: "She isn't the same woman I married." "My husband just doesn't understand me anymore." "I wish we had never married." Some mainline denominations even have a marriage reversal ceremony called "disavowal."

Divorce, according to the late Allan Bloom, is the number-one social problem in America. "Psychologists provide much of the ideology justifying divorce," he wrote. "For example, that it's wrong for kids to stay in stressful homes." One excuse, according to Bloom: "Children may be told over and over again that their parents have a right to their own lives, that they will enjoy quality time instead of quantity time.... Children do not believe any of this."[18]

I realize that taking a strong stand against divorce can be interpreted as judgmental or painting with too broad a stroke. But we have gone too far in accommodating divorce in the Church. In some marital situations, such as abuse, separation is necessary. But we need to view marriage as the covenant relationship God sees it as. The first place to seek guidance is in His Word, which is clear about divorce. God says, "I hate divorce" (Malachi 2:16).

Jesus got to the heart of the matter when He told the Pharisees concerning this issue, "Moses permitted you to divorce your wives because your hearts were hard. But it was not this way from the beginning. I tell you that anyone who divorces his wife, except for marital unfaithfulness, and marries another woman commits adultery" (Matthew 19:8–9).

The world preaches that throwaway marriages are O.K. so long as they promote our own happiness. But God's design for our marriages and broken family relationships is summed up by His desire for restoration rather than alienation.

5. Redefining Life

For women in the United States who choose to abort their unborn babies, January 22, 1973, was supposed to be a day of liberation. On that day the highest court in the land ruled on the now-famous Roe versus Wade case. The Supreme Court determined that it is acceptable to abort a living human fetus up to the twenty-eighth week. Never mind that the unborn child has a functional heart just eighteen weeks after conception. The court ruled against reason. It ruled against nature. Men and women, to appease their consciences, created numerous excuses.

The issue of abortion goes beyond the question of fetal viability—the ability of the fetus to live outside the womb (which comes about much earlier now due to technological advances). If a human being is considered nonviable, it follows that it must not be fully human. So it is that the advocates of a "pro-choice" position have redefined the parameters of human life to soothe their consciences for the sake of convenience.

The excuses for abortion are many. Some women believe there are too many children in the world. Others feel they cannot care properly for a child. Others see the timing as imperfect for bringing a child into the world. And what might happen if the child had some imperfection?

But to accommodate these circumstances, and then to justify them, we must alter the semantics of life. The unborn child may be called tissue but never a human being. Vocabulary modification is the easiest way to avoid the obvious. The euphemism *pro-choice* is another semantic twist. It recognizes only the choice of the person with power, and it gives allegiance to illegitimate power structures through its tacit minimalization of *weaker* human life. Most of all it devalues the helpless carrier-dependent baby inside the womb. Taken to its logical (and extreme) conclusion, such a philosophy dictates that any group, culture or government that is stronger, smarter or more powerful has the right to eliminate those it deems expendable— all for the common good.

6. *What Are You Watching Tonight?*

George Gerbner, dean of communications at the University of Pennsylvania, sees television as "a new and competing religion." It is indeed a major influence shaping the values of our nation. In the average household, television occupies more of our time than anything but sleep. By the time a child reaches eighteen, he or she has spent three full years watching TV. It is the dominant leisure activity of most Americans, consuming forty percent of the average person's free time.[19]

In an article about the influence of the media on teen behavior, Victor Strasburger, chief of the Division of Adolescent Medicine at the University of New Mexico School of Medicine, observes:

> Teenagers watch an average of three hours of TV per day . . . have access to R-rated movies and even pornography long before they are adults. . . . The average American

teenager views almost 15,000 sexual jokes, innuendoes and other references on TV each year. Fewer than 170 (just over 1 percent) of these deal with what any sane adult would define as responsible sexual behavior. . . . Add to that the 20,000 commercials per year each teenager in America sees—with implicit messages that sex is fun, sex is sexy and everyone out there is having sex but you—and you have at least the possibility of a fairly important influence.[20]

Television, satellite programming, videos and movies are more than innocuous leisure activities. Entertainment has become a form of technological idolatry. We reason that we will watch "only the good stuff." But more often than not we flick on the remote and settle in for a few hours of indiscriminate viewing, regardless of moral content.

When the busy housewife pawns her children off on the electronic babysitter, the tube fills her children's imaginations with fantasy and fiction. Their receptive minds are tainted by sacrilegious programming, while many of the positive values that have been implanted within them are systematically deconstructed.

Some women indulge their senses in a kaleidoscope of immoral imagery and visual unreality. Daytime (and nighttime) soaps rob us of time, morality and reality. In this smorgasbord of licentiousness, the heroes are fornicating, cheating, selfish and vain. Viewers confusing fact with fiction cry over relationships that were created in the minds of ungodly scriptwriters. Television drama, we reason, might help us be more caring and compassionate. But Jesus, not television, should fill the emptiness of our lives.

On some weeknights and most weekends, many men consume programs of a different sort. The male soap is the sports program. It carries every bit of the same emotion and squanders just as much time. Sports can be a healthy outlet, but the emphasis we place on it can become idolatrous. This god can steal precious time from family, church and marriage.

Then there is film entertainment. What criteria should Christians use for selecting a movie or video rental? As the rating system becomes more liberal, we get more clever in our excuse-making. A movie provides wholesome diversion, we reason, or it is educational or historical or artistic. Are there circumstances under which it is all right to view an R- or NC-17–rated movie or video? If our thinking is not clear before we click on the cable channel or scan the movie page of the newspaper, we will make a decision for the moment and find it easier to compromise.

One afternoon my wife and I went to a video store to rent a movie. We had never been in the store before and soon noticed it had an X-rated video section. Several minutes later a teenager who attends our church appeared with a stack of pornographic videos. He was surprised. We were shocked. Later the boy's mother, talking with my wife, denied that her son could be responsible for renting the videos. Instead she betrayed the truth by blaming her son's friend.

It is important to guard our minds carefully and stay in touch with what our children consume on their own time.

7. Uploading Fantasy

When Bill was in his late thirties, he grew frustrated with his marriage. He had been raised in a good church in which he eventually became a youth leader. But he had thought marriage would be so different, and his expectations of personal fulfillment had not materialized. Although Bill had a loving wife and two young daughters, he found life dull and uninteresting. His kids got on his nerves and his sex life was a bore.

One evening Bill made a short trip to a local convenience store for milk. On this trip he took more than his usual furtive glance at the slick magazines stacked neatly behind the counter. This time he could not resist the impulse to look inside the glossy cover, so he bought one and tucked it beneath his arm under the gallon of milk.

Bill drove around the corner and pulled discreetly off the road. His ten-minute trip to the store turned into an hour. With heart racing, he thumbed through the pages, scanning the voluptuous bodies of women he longed to have.

On his way home Bill felt more deprived than ashamed. He was careful to hide the magazine in a place where his wife and daughters would not find it. *Maybe it'll help my sex life*, he mused. *At least I'm not hurting anyone. It's not like I'm visiting prostitutes.*

His purchases continued month after month. Eventually he mustered the courage to step inside an adult bookstore. *I'm just a normal, healthy male*, he rationalized to himself.

Then, like many men who give in to sexual addiction, Bill became careless. His wife found a phone bill with hundreds of dollars charged to a sex talk hotline. When she confronted him, Bill became angry and resentful. There was no repentance.

Thousands of men in churches today have the same problem as Bill. They are pastors, deacons, ushers and elders. They are afraid to confess their sin, afraid of rejection—so they adapt. They accept their habit as harmless, normal, even healthy.

In his final interview with Dr. James Dobson, convicted killer Ted Bundy confessed his addiction to pornography. He said it "happened in stages, gradually."[21] The tragedy of Ted Bundy's life and those of his victims could have been avoided had he dealt with his problems early on. But the more we excuse what we do, the easier it is to do it again.

Acting with Reason

Einstein once said, *"Der Herr Gott würfelt nicht"* ("The Lord does not throw dice"). God acts thoughtfully. His moral creatures do, too. So before we talk about the psychology of excuse-making, it is important to reinforce the fact that although we may act under the impulse of strong emotions, we always have our reasons.

The tragic result of excusing wrong choices is that the unconscious mind begins to make adaptations and adjustments. Sociologist C. Wright Mills called this "the trend of rationalization."[22] For the Christian, adhering to worldly values produces spiritual alienation and moral stagnation. One way to remedy this is to begin to view moral absolutes as conditional and try to adapt our beliefs to our behavior.

This cerebral positioning is accompanied by problems. A young man in his twenties is unable to suppress what his conscience tells him is wrong. "Because of my religious beliefs," he says, "I'm supposed to believe that having sex with somebody of the same sex is wrong. Yet I do it frequently, almost every day of my life. The guilt is still there, though." And a woman in her mid-forties says, "Advising my daughter to have an abortion led me to a long suicidal siege. I'm not over it yet. I keep picturing a baby who never existed."

Excuses are designed by the human mind to remove personal responsibility and relieve our consciences. And these excuses always issue out of our wills. Aristotle observed: "Moral excellence or virtue has to do with feelings and actions. These may be voluntary or involuntary. It is only to the former that we assign praise or blame. Nobody encourages us to do things which are not in our power to do and which are not voluntary."[23]

Excuse-making inevitably catches up with us. Like lying—and excuses are a form of lying—others soon find out what we are up to. The person who is perpetually late for appointments can get away with it in the beginning. In fact, the human capacity for forgiveness is strong. When a person is always late, however, and always has an excuse, we begin to see how clever he or she is at coming up with something new.

The residual effects of excuse-making usually concern more than just the excuse-maker. I recall a picture of Senator Brock Adams standing with one arm around his teenage daughter and the other around his wife. His wife, visibly shaken and embarrassed, was fighting back tears. Adams was announcing his withdrawal from the race because he had finally been called to account after years of sexually harassing numerous women. No one who recalls the downfall of Adams or Senator Bob Packwood can say their choices did not hurt others. Their families, supporters and the public were all victims. (Someone must have known Packwood was on a dangerous path. Perhaps his wife was aware of his infidelity. Where were his associates, friends, neighbors or family? Why did they not say something? Were they afraid of the consequences? More about this in chapter 7.)

When we temper our decisions with logic generated by self-interest, we invite self-deception. And we keep self-deception alive when we make or accept excuses for others. We must not allow ourselves to do this. We may reason, *He will never change,* or, *That's just the way she is.* But accepting the dishonesty of others can cause deception to creep slowly into our own lives. And facilitating the misbehavior of others can make it easier for us to engage in wrong behavior ourselves.

The habit of blaming is often reinforced by self-help books, talk shows and therapy. Each of these has an impact on our willingness to see ourselves as victims with good reason to blame others for our problems.

The Psychology of Excuse

We have all been around people who cannot grasp the foolishness of their behavior. It is puzzling. There is the pastor who justifies his lies on the basis of "protecting the flock." There is the mother who excuses the behavior of her delinquent son by saying, "He's a good boy, really." There is the businessman who neglects his family by working eighty-hour weeks, using his family as the reason. How can people believe the lies they tell themselves when others see through their web of deceit?

In 1957 Leon Festinger introduced the theory of cognitive dissonance. Festinger believed that we strive to achieve consistency in all phases of our lives. The "cognitions" include facts, behavior, beliefs, opinions and any other conscious mental processes. When any two of these cognitions are inconsistent, they are in dissonance. The medical doctor who smokes despite his knowledge that smoking causes cancer is in a state of dissonance. His knowledge (cognition) that smoking is harmful to his health is incompatible (dissonant) with his behavior.

A believer who knows that adultery is sinful and yet persists in this behavior has, according to dissonance theory, three alternatives. First, *he or she can add consonant (harmonious) cognitions.* He may say, "God understands my needs." During Jim Bakker's sexual encounter with Jessica Hahn in Florida, he was quoted as saying, "When you help the shepherd, you're helping the sheep."[24] When we use a positive approach to excuse our negative behavior, it helps to reduce the dissonance.

The second alternative is *to change the importance of the dissonant cognitions by making them seem not so bad.* This would be to say, "It isn't the unpardonable sin," or, "We don't live under the law anymore." These people assume they can circumvent sin through human skill or ingenuity. Their excuses, which reduce the negative aspects of what they are doing through the process of justification, diminish the importance of God's Word. As Charles Finney once said, "This is one source of self-deception. Men view the law in the abstract and love it."[25]

The third option is *to change one's cognitions so they are consistent with one's behavior.* We accomplish this in two opposite ways. First, we may adapt to an adulterous affair by declaring, "There's nothing wrong with adultery," and come after a while to accept it as normal. We can thus summarize the connection between dissonance theory and deception with the following statement: *After we make a choice of any value, we will seek justification for that choice.* Or, to make our cognitions consistent with our behavior, we may choose to abandon the troublesome behavior entirely.

Forsaking the sin is, for the Christian, the only acceptable solution to the dilemma of cognitive dissonance. Merely acknowledging one's sin, as I have pointed out, is not enough. As one man told me, "I am a liar. I have been a liar ever since I was a boy, and I'll always be a liar." His recognition of his behavior was not enough to produce a change in his lifestyle. The important element in producing change is recognizing that we will look for justification whenever we make, or are tempted to make, an immoral decision. Dissonance theory predicts that the less external justification there is for an act, the more dissonance will be aroused. Or, we may change our beliefs or attitudes to justify to ourselves the actions we have taken. For Christians, it is a matter of being honest with ourselves and refusing to make or accept any excuses.

When a Christian acts contrary to what he knows is right, he comes face to face with the temptation to compromise his beliefs. This can end in freedom or it can start the process of self-deception. It is at this critical juncture, when faced with wrongdoing, that we must *not* justify ourselves. Unfortunately, many of us take the easy road to reduce dissonance, adjusting our attitudes rather than our behavior.

One of the reasons many Christians experience mental health difficulties is the improper handling of sin. According to social psychologist Michael Saks, "The dissonance produced by two strong, contradictory sets of cognitions creates psychological discomfort which can be tolerated only with difficulty."[26] We must not pass off psychological discomfort as needless condemnation, because the longer we ignore or excuse our behavior, the easier it is to get used to. Often discomfort is the Holy Spirit's warning for us to get our spiritual houses in order. Then and only then can we experience wholeness and healing as our designer intended.

The place to start is with the individual decisions we make every day—at work, in school and in our homes. By making right choices based not on the values of the world but on God's moral law, we will no longer need to manufacture excuses for immoral behavior.

Chapter Highlights

- Excuse-making, by believers as well as unbelievers, is a way of covering sinful choices.
- When we excuse wrong behavior, those excuses serve to free us from responsibility. But excuses do not change the reality of our moral condition.
- In self-deception, excuses are often created by changing the semantics or by applying a more favorable label.
- Ask yourself the following questions: Do I look for ways to reduce guilt other than through confession and restitution? Is there anything I do that has become normal when at first it felt wrong? Do I redefine any of my choices to make them appear more acceptable?
- When excuse-making becomes a habit, it leads to deception in other areas of life. Can you identify any areas of your life in which you have made excuses for poor or sinful decisions?

The Antidote
to Moral Meltdown

In the absence of any objective criteria of right and wrong, good and evil, the self and its feelings become our only moral guide.

Robert Bellah

Obedience is the one qualification for further vision.

G. Campbell Morgan

Jason awoke from his dream. He had never imagined what the world would be like without order. It did not seem possible!

In his dream he had been driving to work. As he backed out of his driveway, a car sped by at twice the posted speed, narrowly missing the fender of Jason's car. *What a jerk*, he thought to himself as he retreated cautiously from the safety of his driveway. He slowed to a stop at the end of his street when he noticed that someone had removed the stop signs. "Vandals," he muttered to himself.

Jason made a right turn onto the busy highway, only to find that the double yellow line separating the traffic was gone. It did not deter him, though. *Everyone knows which side of the road they're supposed to be on,* he said to himself. But as he looked up, a car was headed straight for him. Jason yanked the wheel to the right, then swerved back onto the pavement, as the car nearly collided with him. That was a close call! By now Jason's heartbeat was nearly double its normal rate.

He navigated carefully to the nearby convenience store where he habitually stopped for his first dose of caffeine. But as he approached the store, he noticed double- and triple-parked cars. The patrons whose cars had been boxed in were shouting obscenities at the offenders. Coffee, Jason decided, was not worth the effort.

The bumper-to-bumper traffic he was used to did not seem so bad in retrospect. *Congested streets are better than the chaos of unrestrained freedom,* he reflected as he managed to dodge speeding cars, wrong-way drivers, intersections without lights and streets devoid of markings.

Jason was relieved and shaking when the doors to the elevator at work finally closed behind him. But when he arrived at the fifth floor, only about half his coworkers were there. Those who had made it to work were gathered around a portable radio listening to the morning news. Accidents jammed the expressway. A school bus had been hit at an unmarked rail crossing. Head-on collisions had left shattered glass and broken bodies strewn along the roadways. Worst of all, emergency vehicles could not make it to some sections of the city. Dozens of people had already died waiting for rescue crews to arrive.

Jason sat straight up in his bed. Thank goodness it was only a dream! A world without order was a frightening consideration.

We take order for granted every day. We expect it. We depend on it. Where chaos abounds, poor productivity, destruction and even death rule. A perpetual state of uncertainty causes anxiety and frustration. Places like Lebanon in the 1980s, Bosnia in the mid-1990s and urban war zones scattered throughout the United States come close to fitting this description. A world with no rules, or with no benevolent leader to enforce them, is ruled by anarchy—a world (like the one described in the book of Judges) in which everyone does what is right in his or her own eyes.

Thankfully, God has given His Law to bring order to an otherwise chaotic world, like the one Jason experienced in his dream. The absoluteness and completeness of God's Law leave no doubt about the basis for morality—which is why acknowledging the relevance of His Law is crucial to our moral maturity.

What would you think if you bought a new car and received no owner's manual or instructions for maintaining or operating it? Perhaps you would call the dealer. But what if the salesperson said, "Sorry, your vehicle doesn't come with a manual"?

Happily, that is not the case with the ultimate machine, the human being. The manufacturer has provided an operations manual. (Mine is 1,730 pages thick!) God has given clear instructions about how to operate according to His design. He wisely supplies foundational guidance in this owner's manual: His Law, embodied in the Ten Commandments. He even furnishes examples of owners who did not pay attention to the instructions, in order to help future owners avoid the same maintenance mistakes.

God gave us rules to live by for one reason: He loves us and wants you and me to live according to the way He designed us, so we can take joy in one another and in Him. Robertson McQuilken, author of *Biblical Ethics*, writes, "The owner who follows the instruction manual of the manufacturer is the one who finds satisfaction with the product."[1]

But many owners do not want to trudge through the bulky manual. They feel it is too long and should be condensed. Others feel the manual is too difficult to understand. Some creative people have put the manual on tape,

CD-ROM or on the hard drives of their computers. But because many of these people do not actually read the manual, they wind up repeating the mistakes the instructions are designed to prevent. Some of these owners, when things start to fall apart, even blame the manufacturer for a flawed design.

Whenever we deliberately revise or suppress God's instructions, or live as if there were no laws binding us, we give self-deception fertile ground in which to grow.

Custom-Designed Morality

Aristotle said, "We become just by doing just acts." If the philosopher was right, all we need to do is determine what a just act is, then follow through. And to many of us, the answer is obvious. In America today, however, the lines defining *just acts* are becoming increasingly blurred. We are more likely than ever to underpay our taxes, keep a cash-loaded wallet found on the street[2] or justify cheating in school.[3]

Writers Peter Kim and James Patterson decided to find out just what American moral behavior is like. Here are some of the highlights from their book *The Day America Told the Truth:*

- A third of married men and women confess to having had affairs.
- Just about everyone lies; 91 percent of us lie regularly.
- The majority of Americans (62 percent) say there is nothing wrong with the affairs they are having.
- One in five children lose their virginity before age thirteen.
- About one in four workers are willing to compromise their personal beliefs in order to get ahead on the job.
- Only one in ten believe in all the Ten Commandments.

Kim and Patterson say, "Americans are making up their own rules, their own laws. In fact, we're all making up our own moral codes." They found that a letdown in moral values is now considered the number-one problem facing our country.[4]

Personal morality becomes evident in the choices we make every day. If we determine these moment by moment, we are bound to make decisions generated simply by enlightened self-interest. Medical researcher Dr. Gordon Muir comments, for example, "What has happened in the rush to sexual freedom was not the discovery of a new, free and imaginative society, but the throwing out of necessary codes of conduct for a healthy society."[5] This freedom is illustrated by the advice given by Wisconsin lawyer Debra Koenig to a class of seventh-grade girls: "Sleep around all you want but don't get married."[6]

But just as we cannot violate the manufacturer's instructions for a new car without risking serious problems, neither can we violate God's moral commands without grave repercussions—even physical ones. A study by Johns Hopkins University School of Medicine links unfaithfulness to cervical cancer. Women are five to eleven times more likely to develop this disease if their men frequent prostitutes or have many sexual partners. The risk of cervical cancer is highest for women whose husbands have the most sexual partners. And any woman puts herself at increased risk by having many sexual partners.[7]

Another study by David B. Larson, a medical doctor, helps us understand God's wisdom in giving us the seventh commandment, which is designed to protect the sanctity of marriage. Getting a divorce, Larson found, is only slightly less harmful to your health than smoking a pack of cigarettes per day. The rate of cardiovascular disease for divorced men is twice that of married men. Divorced women die prematurely at higher rates than married women and are more prone to acute conditions such as infectious and parasitic diseases, respiratory illnesses, digestive system illnesses, and severe injuries and accidents. Men and women who divorce are more likely to succumb to substance abuse. Separated or divorced adults are four and a half times more likely to become alcohol-dependent than are married adults. And it comes as little surprise that children of divorce are more likely to drop out of school, suffer from depression and other emotional problems, engage in precocious sexual activity, procreate out of wedlock, get hooked on drugs and alcohol, slip economically below the poverty line, commit suicide and get divorced themselves.[8]

Then there is the custom-designed work ethic. A cover story in *USA Today* titled "Doing the Wrong Thing" described a survey of 1,324 randomly selected workers, managers and executives. Ethical violations are so rampant, the study showed, that if you are not stealing company property, leaking company secrets or lying to customers or supervisors, odds are the worker next to you is. Nearly half of all workers admit to having taken unethical or illegal actions in the past year. Constant violations have made workers so callous that deception passes for good stewardship.[9]

Unethical conduct has become so acceptable that it is finding its way into advertising. In a recent marketing campaign by Schweitzer Mountain Resort, one of the best skiing areas in the Northwest just a short drive from my home in north Idaho, bumper stickers and billboards read *Call in Sick* with a picture of a skier taking a run down the mountain. The creator of Schweitzer's advertising campaign apparently did not care about the long-term implications of the campaign. But if resort employees took the advertising at face value, there would be no one to run the lifts or operate the food service! And other area employers did not voice their concern for how Schweitzer was encouraging both lying and employee absence.

But such behavior has become normal. A survey shows that the more sick leave companies give employees, the more days they call in sick,[10] even though calling in sick when one is not sick is a theft of time. The overall cost of unreported employee theft was estimated recently at $120 billion a year.

The reason we are facing moral meltdown is that we revere personal comfort or advancement above doing what is right. Even the phrase *doing what is right*, like Aristotle's *just acts*, carries different meanings for many people. Doing the right thing is simply doing what makes the most sense for them personally. Except now we are finding out how redefining morality has affected our marriages, businesses, government, family, schools and relationships.

The origin and legitimizing of excuse-making (which we looked at in the last chapter) and the foundation of moral meltdown are planted firmly in the social sciences. I want to show how these ideas have crept into the Church and into much of our own thinking.

Masters of Blame: Scientific Fallacies

Secular humanity yearns to create a new and presumably better set of moral criteria that will usher in a brave new world. The structures imposed by "fundamentalists"— those who believe in the truth of God's Word and cling to it uncompromisingly—ostensibly have no relevance. New problems require sophisticated scientific solutions. So, rather than rely on the certainty of God's moral law, men and women formulate their own truths. They pride themselves on the empirical, the testable and the factual. They are slaves to the scientific method. For them it is the new Enlightenment.

Scientific and religious determinists imply that external factors compel us to act. When we accept this premise, it is easier to rationalize past or future behavior on the grounds of *inability*. This path of least resistance is what those in self-deception choose most often. The problem is that when our behavior ceases to be volitional and emerges as the product of environmental causes, we must reexamine the very basis of our society, such as the penal code. If a criminal is simply the byproduct of uncontrollable causes, we cannot justly hold him accountable for his actions.

The fact is, in the arena of personal choice and responsibility, we cannot rely on science to serve as our guide to moral truth or social rehabilitation. If we do, we become bound to that which has its roots in empiricism. While we live in a world that relies on the empirical, to venerate it as a panacea for our societal problems is to distort reality. German physicist Werner Heisenburg once said, "I am now convinced that scientific truth is unassailable in its own field. I have never found it possible to dismiss the content of religious thinking as simply a part of an outmoded phase in the consciousness of mankind."[11]

When we serve the Baal of empiricism, we omit the preeminence of moral truth. When we view God's Law as anything less than transcendent reality, we start down the path to moral ambiguity characterized by self-deception. For the Christian, the emasculation of God's Word gradually produces a willingness to compromise. And when we deprecate the moral law, it claims no authority over our actions.

Objective and permanent truths about human behavior do not evolve out of scientific observation, nor from hypotheses provable through controlled observation and verification. The champions of human prediction believe that the relative newness of behavioral science explains much of its feebleness in forecasting. *But the science of human prediction cannot forecast with absolute certainty.* It is the existence of freedom that is a prerequisite for moral behavior. As Walter Stace wisely noted:

Morality is concerned with what men ought and ought not to do. But if man has no freedom to choose what he will do, if whatever he does, is done under compulsion, then it does not make sense to tell him that he ought not to have done what he did and he ought to do something different . . . if he acts under compulsion, how can he be held morally responsible for his actions?[12]

The Purpose of the Law

> You can never change the way people feel; let them do just what they will.
>
> George Michael, singer

The notion that God's laws bring freedom often produces a chuckle. In reality, we believe the Law does just the opposite: It puts us in bondage. We view the Law as restrictive or inhibiting (although this is clearly not what the Israelites thought). For many of us, the Ten Commandments are outdated. They were God's customized plan for the Israelites and are not relevant for us. So it is that many Christians insist, "We no longer live under the law."

R. J. Rushdoony challenges this mindset:

> The purpose of grace is not to set aside the law but to fulfill the law and enable men to keep the law. If the law is so serious in God's sight that it would require the death of Jesus Christ, the only begotten Son of God, to make atonement for man's sin, it seems strange for God to then proceed to abandon the law.[13]

Christ's death on the cross abolished the ceremonial laws. No longer do we need to sacrifice animals for our sins. Jesus Christ fulfilled this requirement once and for all. But His death did not abolish the moral law. The *function* of the Law is to show us how sinful (or off the moral mark) we are. But this is not the *reason* God gave us the Law. We get this important distinction confused.

If God gave us the Law simply to show us how sinful we are, that would not give us much motivation to behave according to its dictates. But God tells us *why* He gave us the moral law: "The LORD commanded us to observe all these statutes, to fear the LORD our God *for our good always* and for our survival" (Deuteronomy 6:24, NASB, emphasis added). Our Designer is trying to tell us that true freedom comes through living according to the way He made us. And it is not our inability to obey His commands that makes us guilty, but our *unwillingness* to obey. The apostle Paul tells us to "count yourselves dead to sin. . . . Do not offer the parts of your body to sin . . . for sin shall not be your master" (Romans 6:11, 13–14).

God's Word teaches us, then, that we must master our sin—and this is an act of the will:

> "This commandment which I command you today is not too difficult for you, nor is it out of reach. It is not in heaven, that you should say, 'Who will go up to heaven for us to get it for us and make us hear it, that we may observe it?' . . . But the word is very near you, in your mouth and in your heart, that you may observe it."
>
> Deuteronomy 30:11–12, 14, NASB

Wholly Holy

There is an unmistakable correlation between the Law and personal holiness. Holiness means "to be separate." When God says, "Be holy because I, the LORD your God, am holy" (Leviticus 19:2), He is saying, "Be different from everybody else."

Holiness is not sinlessness, but it *is* less sinning. Our love for God and our separation from the sinful influences of the world naturally mean we will make fewer sinful choices. Holiness has to do with motive—why we do what we do.

Ask yourself this question: Is it possible to evaluate a person's intentions by the actions he or she chooses? Suppose I tell you I am planning to run a marathon in six months. You may respond by saying, "I hope you do well," or, "I think you're nuts!" Either way, my subordinate choices will tell you how serious I really am. If I fail to train for the marathon, would it be judgmental of you to assume I am not very serious about it? Of course not. You would be exercising a bit of deductive reasoning. If I train regularly, on the other hand, it would be unfair for you to assume I have no plans to run.

In the same way, the quality of our moral decisions is played out in our lives every day. Do I love God? If so, my actions will attest to my love for Him. Do I care about my family? My behavior will support my claim. Do I love my wife? Do I care about others? The answers to these questions are not difficult to determine. In each case the truth is dictated by my behavior. Likewise our holiness is a product of our choices, which in turn produce moral behavior.

Yet this is not what some believers teach. Author Kent Wilson argues that we are holy already. "Be what you are," he writes. "You are holy; now be that way and live that way."[14] But what *are* we, and how can we know for sure? Are we Christians because we accept a label, or do we show we are Christians because our conduct is different? If you put on a New York Yankees uniform, does that make you a New York Yankee? Of course not. A professional baseball player with a signed contract is entitled to wear a uniform because of his skill on the field. In fact, his performance during games testifies to other players about his quality as a ballplayer. His own actions judge him.

The same thing is true for Christians. We do not become holy by repeating the sinner's prayer. There is nothing magical about saying those words. Nor does one become a good spouse by saying, "I do" at the altar. Holiness, like obedience to God's laws, is the result of a series of choices to serve and please our Designer. And it is the human will that links the law to holiness.

But our relationship with God goes much deeper. In a world in which lawlessness abounds, separation from the world is a necessity. It means we become a "peculiar people" (1 Peter 2:9, KJV). *Peculiar* in this sense means "belonging exclusively to one person or group." Holiness is God's way of saying, "Don't mingle with the world and don't participate in its behavior." It is a general statement of condition. Through the Law God is saying, "Let Me show you how to behave." The moral law is a specific statement about how to operate our machinery in a morally polluted world.

Now here is the reason this discussion about holiness and the Law is so crucial. The person in self-deception tends to see the moral law as extraneous to faith. His or her theology—what he thinks about God—emanates from a warped interpretation of the Bible. And one of the first elements of God's Word to be dismantled is the moral law. Why? Because the Law serves as a divider, separating the law-abiding from the lawless. As these lines blur, the self-deceived are better able to justify their behavior. And eliminating the relevance of the moral law makes it easier to engage in immorality.

Upholding God's Absolutes

The sage Obe-Wan-Knobe says to Luke Skywalker in the film *Return of the Jedi*, "You are going to find out that many of the truths that we cling to depend upon your own point of view." In just that way, the overwhelming majority of people in our country believe they are qualified to determine what is or is not moral. Fully 93 percent, according to Patterson and Kim, base their moral decisions on their own experience. Those authors ask, "What's right?

What's wrong? When you are making up your own rules, your own moral codes, it can make the world a pretty confusing place."[15]

According to a Barna research poll, 71 percent of U.S. adults say there is no such thing as absolute truth.[16] A lecture given by Professor Arthur Schlesinger at Brown University demonstrates the penchant our society has for disregarding absolutes. He called them "the great enemy today in the life of the mind." According to Schlesinger, "Relativism is the American way. . . . The mystic prophets of the absolute cannot save us. . . . We must save ourselves."[17]

Herbert Schlossberg in his book *Idols for Destruction* takes a different point of view:

> Man strives to become the autonomous ruler of himself, able to define right and wrong and to frame statutes according to whatever he defines as just. Or else man is created and sustained by a holy and just God who declares on matters of right and wrong in the form of the law.[18]

Ravi Zacharias, a modern-day prophet and scholar, refers to the "autonomous culture" and defines a place where

> every individual is self-determining and independent of authority. Morality imposed from without is resisted, and intuition as grounds for belief is optional. In short, autonomous cultures deny any moral authority and shrug their shoulders at intuition.[19]

We are fast becoming—if we have not become so already—the autonomous culture Zacharias talks about. Worse yet, this culture has its origins (as we have seen) in the deification of individualism and the shucking off of transcendent moral codes to guide us. We have put ourselves on moral autopilot, and the settings are drastically off. At least part of the reason for this state of affairs has to do with the Church's laxity toward the moral law.

Many in the Church have a name for people who take the moral law too seriously. They dismiss them as legalists, and the morally indulgent on both sides of the fence view moralist expectations as unreasonably high, unrealistic or downright impossible. But God is not looking for people to rewrite His manual or provide condensed versions of His Word. He is seeking men and women who will stand for the truth of Scripture without compromise. He wants courageous believers willing to stand out in a world shaded in gray.

Psychiatrist Karl Menninger was one who viewed the maintenance of morality as chiefly the responsibility of the Church:

> The clergyman cannot minimize sin and maintain his proper role within our culture. We need him as our umpire to direct us, to accuse us, to reproach us, to intercede for us, to shrive us [hear confession and offer absolution]. Failure to do so is his sin.[20]

Moral intervention is not an easy task. The clergy can lose followers by being too tough on sin. It is easier to do nothing or to leave the job to a higher authority. If it gets too bad, we reason, God will intervene.

Shrinking in the face of sin is not a new problem. In his lecture "The Decay of Conscience," nineteenth-century evangelist Charles Finney wrote:

> [The clergy] fail to go to the bottom of the matter and insist upon obedience to the moral law as alone acceptable to God. They hold a different standard from that which is inculcated in Christ's sermon on the mount, which was Christ's exposition of the moral law. He expressly taught there was no salvation without conformity to the rule of

life laid down in that sermon. True faith will always and inevitably beget a holy life.[21]

While church leaders do indeed lead the way for the rest of us, we cannot lay all the fault at their feet. Each of us reinvents the Law of God every time we refuse to uphold the absoluteness of His Law in our own lives. When we justify immoral behavior, either our own or someone else's, we are telling the manufacturer that we know more about the design of the product than He does.

Instead of looking for ways around the clear injunctions of God's Word, we should do everything we can to reinforce His purposes and design for our lives. And, nearly as important, we must teach our children and grandchildren the wisdom of and reasons for living our lives in submission to God.

God's Early Warning System

The great Norwegian long distance runner Grete Waitz once commented, "Pain is telling you something. Don't shut out its message by trying to cover it up." When God assembled you and me, He included a diagnostic warning system called pain. When we ignore pain, serious consequences ensue.

God designed us with another unique system that operates on the same principle of pain. This mechanism, called the conscience, acts as an alarm, warning us of moral danger. It is like a warning light on the control panel of your car. It is there to tell you when something is wrong. You can choose to ignore the red light and suffer the consequences to your engine, or you can fix the problem. It is the same with the conscience. As Christians we are responsible to obey the truth of God's Word. God says, "To one who knows the right thing to do, and does not do it, to him it is sin" (James 4:17, NASB). If we choose to disregard the truth, we will begin to feel guilty. Menninger referred to this as a form of self-punishment. "The mounting internal stress of unrelieved conscience," he wrote, "disturbs the equilibrium and organization of the personality."[22]

Guilt, contrary to popular opinion, is simply the byproduct of failing to fix a problem. "People who reject Biblical doctrines of responsibility and sin," says Schlossberg, "do not thereby rid themselves of guilt. They do, however, rid themselves of any way to handle their guilt."[23] Happily, God's instruction manual tells us how to reduce guilt and prevent damage to ourselves and others. This comes about through confessing sin, forsaking it and making restitution. These repair systems were designed for our spiritual, physical and emotional well-being. God's Word tells us to "confess your sins to each other" (James 5:16). It also tells us why confession is important: "So that you may be healed." The healing God wants to give us is emotional and spiritual. In other words, it is moral.

A disproportionate number of Christians are in therapy, as I pointed out in the last chapter, as the direct result of unsettled transgressions. These may be the result of our own sin or past sins against us. So before we rush off to mental health professionals or begin taking prescription drugs, we should look at this often-neglected area called the conscience. The Christian with extreme anxiety, depression or phobias should first examine his or her conscience:

- Is there an area of my life in which I have not lived as God designed me to live?
- Do relations with family members need to be mended?
- Am I ignoring the pleading of the Holy Spirit in some area of my life?

There is danger when a pastor or counselor provides false comfort or faulty solutions to someone who needs to repent or restore or make restitution. It is possible to use techniques to soothe a conscience that needs to be uncovered and renewed. In some instances, rather than provide long-term help, a counselor may actually inhibit the work God is trying to do in a person's life.

This is a tricky area because the Church must not neglect emotional hurts. The victims of sexual or emotional abuse need our compassion and care. But some with self-destructive attitudes are harboring bitterness, resentment or an unwillingness to forgive. These attitudes require spiritual healing, and the conscience plays an important role in pestering people until they get things right. Although it seems good to show compassion to those we perceive are hurting, when we do so unconditionally, without understanding the reasons for the hurt, we can be acting in compassionate ignorance and making a bad situation worse.

What Happens When We Don't Listen?

If people continue to sin and ignore guilt over a long time, it begins to dissipate. Have you ever been so tired in the morning that you did not hear your alarm clock? Suddenly you realize you have overslept, and the race is on to make it to work or school. Some of us ignore the alarm purposely, punching the snooze button over and over until the noise has little effect on us.

The same can happen with the conscience. Ignoring it does two things. First, it dulls us to the seriousness of sinful behavior. Second, it begins to rot away our consciences from the inside. It happens in the same way that atmospheric pollutants break down the ozone layer, creating a gaping hole that enables harmful substances to get through. The Bible calls it having the conscience "seared as with a hot iron" (1 Timothy 4:2). The notion behind the term *sear* is that where the searing takes place, we are no longer able to feel. This leads to a hardening or callousness of heart, and God's Word starts to have little or no effect on us.

Have you ever watched a gymnast on the rings or uneven bars? The constant friction would burn blisters into your hands and mine if we could do the same movements. Yet the gymnast feels nothing. She goes about her routine without even thinking about the skin on her hands. The searing of our conscience is like the gymnast's calluses. As we keep repeating a particular behavior, we do not feel much after a while, but begin to accept and believe that our excuses are plausible. And when we violate the conscience, God's early warning system, the results are subtle but lead to disaster. Ignoring God's clear instructions (as we saw with King Saul) is one of the steps that leads to self-deception.

Coming Out of Hibernation

Unless the Church stands firm against the rising tide of secularism and immorality, we will regard traditional forms of biblical morality as excessively harsh or restrictive. We will do this for the sake of expediency or the desire to be like everyone else. Those who become acclimated to changing trends within a corrupt culture inevitably become outsiders with God. These cultural adaptations are now influencing nearly every aspect of the North American Church. Attitudes toward marriage, sexuality, abortion and entertainment are flexing with the trend toward gentle accommodation. The character played by screen actor Marlon Brando in the film *The Island of Dr. Moreau* could have been speaking to the Church when he said, "We've surrendered our lives to the momentum of mediocrity."

I remember standing at the top of the amphitheater of the once-prosperous city of Laodicea. Located in present-day western Turkey, Laodicea was a wealthy Roman market town known for banking, wool products and pharmaceuticals. The people were comfortable, secure. They needed nothing. But today this city on the plains of Asia Minor, resembling a ghost town, is only a dim reminder of the affluence of the past. As I stood among the tall weeds growing everywhere, I recalled the words of Jesus to this ancient church:

> "I know your deeds, that you are neither cold nor hot. I wish you were either one or the other! So, because you are lukewarm—neither hot nor cold—I am about to spit you out of my mouth. . . . I counsel you to buy from me gold refined in the fire, so you can become rich."
>
> Revelation 3:15–16, 18

We must learn to love righteousness, to hate sin, to put our efforts into what will last eternally instead of wasting time on the temporal, or trying to make wrong become right. We may genuinely believe, as King Saul did, that the position and values we defend are in line with God's. We can feed these distorted self-belief systems by accepting doctrinal imbalance. Those in self-deception, like the Pharisees, may use God's name as if He were a close friend. Others simply place the blame elsewhere. But if the Church is to be the standard-bearer of truth and righteousness, we must find a way out of our moral hibernation.

In Part 2 of this book, we will look in specific ways at how the neglect of truth can play out in our lives. First let's identify certain specific character qualities among those who are most susceptible to self-deception. While the listing in the following chapter is not intended to be exhaustive, it will help us see the traits that develop as a result of moral compromise.

Chapter Highlights

- The basis for morality is the moral law. Its purpose is to help us live as God designed us, in unity with

Him and with one another, and its warnings are for our good. How well do you know His Law? Do you meditate on it as King David did?

- Our society, spurning God's Law, has redefined morality according to a different set of criteria.
- Holiness, like obedience to God's laws, is the result of a series of choices to serve and please our Designer.
- The conscience is an early warning system designed to keep us from covering over transgressions instead of confessing and repenting of them.
- When we ignore the message of the conscience, we gradually become immune to its warnings, and self-deception takes root in our lives.

PART 2

The Mechanics of Compromise

The Symptoms of Compromise

Allowing and encouraging ambiguity is one way we engage in self-deception.

Professor Sidney Callahan

As behavior worsens, the community adjusts its standards so conduct once thought reprehensible is no longer deemed so.

Robert H. Bork

My phone rang late one evening. It was a friend from the Midwest. For the next hour Cynthia Willis (not her real name) poured out her heart. Her husband, Jonathan, a graduate of a solid Christian school and now a doctor, was having an affair with a nurse at the hospital he worked in.

"Have you been to see your pastor?" I asked.

"Yes, but Jonathan doesn't think what he's doing is such a big deal. He says he loves her." Then in desperation she exclaimed, "Something's wrong with him! He just doesn't care how I feel."

As I comforted Cynthia, I realized that Jonathan, like others in self-deception, was becoming morally blind.

God's Word says, "Each one is tempted when he is carried away and enticed by his own lust. Then when lust has conceived, it gives birth to sin . . ." (James 1:14–15, NASB). This passage provides some important insight. First, it is our lust that produces fertile ground for the seed of sin. The word *lust* simply means "too strong a desire." When we sin, it is usually the result of unresolved longing within our hearts. The combination of opportunity plus desire gives birth to sin.

When we give birth to a child, we cannot give it back again. It becomes a living reality. When we conceive sin, it works the same way. This is the reason we need to stop lust in our minds before it gives birth to action.

I was curious how Jonathan, a devout Christian, could be so casual about adultery. Where was the seed that had given birth to his sin? Here is what I learned from Cynthia. Several months before his adulterous affair started, he bought a subscription to a cable service. Late at night, after their two children were asleep, he and Cynthia watched X-rated programs together. At first she was reluctant. Finally he convinced her that watching pornographic programs would help their sex life. Instead it created an unrealistic appetite that neither of them could legitimately fulfill.

Jonathan, like many who rationalize their sin, was becoming callous. As Cynthia saw it, he no longer cared about what was right. The truth of God's Word was no longer as important as feeding his appetite. His feelings had surfaced as the supreme ruler in his life. And although he had always been caring and compassionate, Cynthia's deep hurt now elicited little concern in him. (Jonathan tells his own story in some detail in the appendix, "Breaking Free: A Case Study.")

Whenever a Christian becomes hardened to his sin, it is difficult for him to see moral issues with much objectivity. While many continue in their religious routine, most do not recognize their own detachment or lack of concern.

Their outward actions—going to church, reading the Bible, praying—mask the reality of their condition and become a mechanism to appraise themselves spiritually. They still *look* healthy.

But the external form of godliness is counterfeit spirituality. The apostle Paul spoke of people who, like the Pharisees, have "a form of godliness but [deny] its power" (2 Timothy 3:5), and he cautioned Timothy to have nothing to do with them. Although we may find comfort in maintaining outward piety, inside we are full of "dead men's bones" (Matthew 23:27).

Jonathan exhibited many of the dominant characteristics of those in self-deception—traits to which we now turn our attention. While the labels are useful, it is important to explain that not everyone in deception has all these traits. Conversely, some people *not* in deception display some of these qualities. A label is useful if it helps us distinguish a good product from an inferior one. It is through recognizing these characteristics in ourselves and others that wholeness and healing can result. If we ignore them, we become prime candidates for self-deception.

Pride: The Source of Rebellion

We saw earlier that the root of all sin and deception is pride. Pride is the source of all other sins because it displaces God as the legitimate ruler of our lives. Pride not only blinds us to our own condition, but it disables us and makes us ineffective in dealing with the pain or needs of others.

The correlation to deception is clear. A proud person believes that his or her opinions and actions are right. A person who is proud refuses correction or reproof. He guards himself from incoming criticism.

If we cannot receive discipline from another believer, we probably will not accept it from the Lord. And when we deny the conviction of the Holy Spirit in our lives, we also deny the potency of the Gospel. It is only through conviction of sin that the Gospel produces fruit in our lives. When we refuse the Holy Spirit, we actually stop growing spiritually. Perhaps you know someone who does not seem to be making much progress in his or her walk with the Lord. This happens when we refuse access to the Holy Spirit in some area of our lives. It cuts us off from further revelation.

As Christians we should never stop growing, maturing and learning. Jesus said, "Every tree that does not bear good fruit is cut down and thrown into the fire" (Matthew 7:19). We must not shut ourselves off from the beckoning of the Spirit, our consciences, God's Word or fellow believers.

One result of pride, as we will see, is the frightening extent to which many will go to guard their image. When people are willing to manipulate, deceive or control others to conceal their own sin, they are in self-deception.

Willingness to Listen but Not to Change

"Reprove one who has understanding and he will gain knowledge" (Proverbs 19:25, NASB). One qualification for further truth is a willingness to learn. When we obey the truth of God's Word, we will grow. We should pray as King David prayed: "Show me your ways, O LORD, teach me your paths" (Psalm 25:4). But the effect of pride is often resistance to moral truth. None of us likes correction. When we refuse reproof, however, we are bound to maintain a false impression of ourselves.

Don't be fooled by appearances. When we recognize we have a problem, it is not the same as doing something to correct it. I know many people (I mentioned one in the last chapter) who have been willing to admit they needed help. Some of them were like the rich young ruler, unwilling to do what was necessary to become Christ's disciple.

Further, a person's presence in counseling can be a smokescreen designed to project an image of spiritual openness.

Effective counseling should produce some change in thinking or behavior. The only reliable test to determine the effectiveness of counseling is a change in action. For those in deception, the symbol of their "godliness" can be their willingness to receive counseling.

Willingness to go for help may be a healthy sign, but it does not in itself certify a willing heart to receive help.

Defending Moral Dishonor

Our response to sin must be like that of King David: "It is against you and you alone I sinned, and did this terrible thing" (Psalm 51:4, TLB). God's Word should not elicit a defensive response in us. As the Holy Spirit bears witness to our hearts and convicts us of sin, our reaction ought to be one of godly sorrow. Can you imagine King David telling the prophet Nathan, "Who do you think you are? I can hear from God just as well as you can!"

The searchlight of the Holy Spirit often shines most where we prefer things to stay hidden. How can we deal with our sin adequately if we guard ourselves from seeing it? The cost to David, as we have seen, was enormous. But an honest Christian is one who seeks truth regardless of the cost. We should delight to know the truth because it enables us to gain a clearer view of our Savior. Those wary of self-disclosure are often hiding something. Yet Jesus always brought into light the hidden thoughts of the heart. He did it with the woman at the well, the rich young ruler, His own disciples. He wants to do the same with you and me.

Control: Keeping the Lid On

The need to control others or situations to our advantage has been called a compulsive behavior. Controllers have more anxiety, more fear, more insecurity and more anger. There is always a big gap between what controlling people want and what they have.[1] They often refuse to follow rules and, unless they are leaders, they regard superiors as obstacles. They are afraid to be exposed for who or what they are, and they will go to almost any lengths to protect their image.

The motivating force behind many controlling people is either pride or insecurity. When we control others we are saying, "I know what's best for me *and* for you." The controller has to have his or her own way. When he cannot get it, he either becomes melancholic or has a tantrum. The "triplets" of pride, control and manipulation often operate in tandem, becoming the way a person controls a situation. This way he can keep a lid on his sinful behavior.

Our control keeps God from taking command in our lives. Like pride, it is a form of self-worship. It is a violation of the first commandment: "You shall have no other gods before me" (Exodus 20:3). We cannot give up control and keep control of our lives at the same time. Remember Jesus asking, "Why do you call me, 'Lord, Lord,' and do not do what I say?" (Luke 6:46).

When we make Jesus the Master of our lives, He requires that we surrender control to Him. As our Designer and Creator, God want us to trust Him since He alone knows what is best for us. He wants us to allow His Spirit to shape us. But this cannot happen when we try to keep control. Whenever we try to govern our own lives, we are conveying our lack of confidence in God and preventing Him from working.

Insecurity: The Two-Edged Sword

Insecurity might be called either the great motivator or the terrible inhibitor. It either shatters our self-confidence, leaving us disabled, or it stimulates us to action out of fear of failure.

There is a healthy measure of insecurity in all of us. We recognize our mortality, and most of us acknowledge limits to our knowledge, power and understanding. But we mask our insecurities through education, dress, buying habits, work, anger, control or any number of ways.

The person in self-deception does not want anyone to remind him of his deficiencies. He may be willing to admit them, but he is not interested in dealing with them. That would be too painful. The person in deception may also fear that someone will uncover his hidden secrets. But this is exactly what God wants to happen! He wants us to depend on and trust in Him alone for our security. When we do this, the method we choose to accomplish a task will be in line with God's will and purpose.

Insecurity incapacitates us and prevents us from moving forward as God desires. But our willingness to share our fears or failures with one another can release the grip insecurity has over us. This is one reason the Bible encourages us to "confess [our] sins to each other" (James 5:16).

The Decay of Reason: A Growing Imbalance

As a person falls deeper into self-deception—I will explain the stages in the next chapter—his ability to think reasonably about his activity begins to diminish. Although this is particularly common in extramarital affairs, sin of any kind throws us off-balance emotionally, spiritually and mentally. We might compare this imbalance to that of a person caught in the grip of a cult. It is nearly impossible to use reason alone to release that person from bondage.

The person in deception is under a similar delusion. Persistence in evading the truth of God's Word distorts the person's perception of reality. Jeremiah wrote,

O LORD, do not your eyes look for truth? You struck them, but they felt no pain; you crushed them, but they refused correction. They made their faces harder than stone and refused to repent.

Jeremiah 5:3

As we harden our hearts, we become unwilling to see our immorality for what it is. And the twisting of truth eventually dampens our moral sensibility.

"The longer we continue to make wrong decisions," wrote Erich Fromm, "the more our heart hardens; and the more we make right decisions, the more our heart softens."[2]

Compromise: No Middle Ground

We have discussed how people in self-deception compromise behavior they know to be wrong. This is a major characteristic that has begun to infiltrate many churches and denominations today. Any of us can make wrong seem right. When we do this long enough, we become masters of compromise. Our deception hinges on our believability to ourselves and to others. We produce clever explanations for every action. We may even recite Scripture to back our claims.

If a person wants to do something badly enough, he will find a way to justify it. This, as you can see, is where compromise becomes a serious issue for the Christian. The compromiser becomes the justifier and the justifier becomes the deceived.

Moral compromise is sin. And when we compromise in small areas of our lives, it becomes easier to compromise in larger ones. If it is O.K. to lie to get out of a dinner engagement, why not lie to a client about the quality of a product? If it is all right to lie at work, why not lie to our children or spouses? The discerning Christian recognizes the progressive nature of compromise and refuses to use it no matter what it costs. This is not legalism; it is moral integrity.

Doctrinal Selectivity

There is nothing new about using God's Word for selfish or sinful purposes. During a meeting with clergy and laymen in Clermont-ferrand, France, in 1095, Pope Urban II gave a rousing discourse to his audience. The congregation is said to have responded enthusiastically with the words *Deus vult*, "God wills it." These two words provided justification to Christians across Western Europe to declare holy war on the Turks. The Crusaders, frustrated by constant setbacks, eventually wrested control of Jerusalem from the infidels and slaughtered thousands of Jews, Arabs and Turks mercilessly in their ostensible zeal for God.

Those in deception search the Scripture for heroes of the faith whose sin "justifies" their own. For the adulterer it is David. For the backslider it is Peter. For the drunkard it is Noah. Deceived people also focus on only a handful of God's attributes, stressing His mercy, grace, longsuffering and forgiveness and ignoring His jealousy, justice and judgment. Yet when we dissect the character of God, choosing those elements of His character that suit us, we distort who God is by making Him into the image we want Him to be.

Be wary of anyone who uses the Word of God to rationalize behavior choices you know are contrary to His Word. Like the Pharisees, they may look religious, but they pervert the truth of God. Likewise, take care yourself not to use Bible verses out of context to support an excessive drinking habit, misplaced anger, overwork or anything else that does not measure up to Scripture.

Comforting Associations

I know a woman in her mid-thirties who has been contemplating divorce for several years. She goes to a fine church and attends a Bible study every week. She has most of the comforts that an upper-class woman could dream of. She surrounds herself with compassionate friends and visits her psychiatrist every week. Her sympathetic sage advises her, "Seek your own happiness. Leave him; think of yourself. Life is too short."

When troubled spouses are surrounded by so much sympathy and support, it comes as little surprise when another marriage begins to crumble.

Christians in deception search for allies, preferably other believers who think and act as they do, to ease their consciences. They support each other during times of moral failure. Indeed, it is human nature to find comfort anywhere we can. Yet the warning for us all is to be careful where we seek comfort when we are in sin. When a person looks for consolation in dissolving his marriage, where does he go? To the happily married? No, usually to someone with "understanding and compassion," someone "who really understands."

If we are seekers of the truth, our relationships will include those willing to tell us the truth, as the prophet Nathan did David, rather than a network of loyalists or moral yes men to sustain us in our deception. Ask yourself whether consensus, friends or peers have replaced what you know to be morally true. A true friend confronts because he or she loves. To *avoid* confrontation because of love is not love at all.

Exerting Unholy Influence

A person in self-deception not only looks for those who agree with him, but tries to convince others to see things his way. When we are in sin, we have a strong desire to encourage others to see our choices in a better light. If these choices are immoral, and we are interacting with someone important to us, the pressure we exert can be intense.

But whenever we try to influence others to see our immorality as "not so bad," we put ourselves in a risky position. Jesus referred to the religious leaders as "blind guides of the blind. And if a blind man guides a blind man, both will fall into a pit" (Matthew 15:14, NASB). Jesus used some of the strongest language in the New Testament to expose those who influence people away from God instead of toward Him, those who lure others into sin. He said of such a person, "It would be better for him to have a large millstone hung around his neck and to be drowned in the depths of the sea" (Matthew 18:6).

Many times in Israel's history the Word speaks of exerting unholy influence. For example: "[The king] did evil in the eyes of the LORD, walking in the ways of his father and in his sin, which he had caused Israel to commit" (1 Kings 15:26). When we are in deception, our choices influence our children, our peers and other believers negatively. God wants us to influence one another for righteousness.

Diversion from Reality

Four out of five Americans live in cities. These surroundings create depersonalization, loneliness, even frenzy. French sociologist Emile Durkheim coined the term *anomie* to describe this state of affairs. He defined the results of anomie as a general breakdown in norms. The anomic person, although encircled by people, feels a sense of detachment from society. Urbanization, ironically, breeds isolation, despair and lawlessness. And busy cities, in which there is movement, noise and incessant activity, create an exaggerated state of agitation. This heightened pace of life can be addictive for some.

What does this have to do with self-deception? A person in deception is drawn to any place, person or activity that will occupy his mind or time. This keeps him from having to deal with the important issues of life.

As we become busier, it is easier to slip into an ends-justify-the-means mentality. Anomie can also foster insecurity. The person in deception reduces his insecurity through activity, since busyness is one way he feels valuable to God or himself. The more he does, the better he feels about himself. But God is interested not in what we can achieve on our own; He is interested in whether we will obey Him. He wants to divert us long enough to get us back to reality.

Lack of Genuine Accountability

Accountability has become a buzzword in the 1990s. What exactly is it? In simple terms, accountability means there are people in your life and mine who are able to set us back on course.

It is possible, of course, for our accountability to be in word only. Likewise, there are some people who are accountable only on paper. The person in deception answers to no one but himself on matters of importance. He is perfectly willing to be accountable when there is no disagreement about what he is to be accountable for. He may put up a good front to outsiders, and he will almost certainly admit he is accountable to God. But when someone suggests that his behavior is inappropriate, he can become angry or defensive.

He may use manipulation, control or wit to get his way. He will generally do whatever it takes to keep control. He wants nothing standing between him and his sin. Regardless of what he says, he is not living in accountability to other Christians, to his pastor or even to God.

This lack of genuine accountability undermines the Church's vitality. In many instances, when accountability becomes an issue within a local fellowship, people look for a new place to attend. One way we can tell when someone is truly accountable is to watch how he handles a situation in which he must submit to a higher authority—any authority following the dictates of God's Word without compromise. When a believer is reluctant to do this, he or she is not walking in accountability.

Loss of Discernment

Discernment is the ability to separate or distinguish correctly. We develop it through knowing and habitually obeying God's Word. "Solid food is for the mature, who by constant use have trained themselves to distinguish good from evil" (Hebrews 5:14). We will talk about discernment later in the book. But for now, note that the person in self-deception changes the absoluteness of God's Word to the extent that his or her moral vision becomes blurred. This may not affect every area of his life, but it will influence some areas of his life. He does not see many moral issues as clearly as he should.

It is only through learning to discern truth from error that we can protect ourselves from false teaching or the influence of others. Our discernment skills also protect us from apostasy. Paul warns us to "examine everything carefully; hold fast to that which is good" (1 Thessalonians 5:21, NASB). Paul also says, "In later times some will fall away from the faith, paying attention to deceitful spirits and doctrines of demons" (1 Timothy 4:1, NASB). These doctrines can be anything that divert our hearts and attention from the truth of God's Word.

The person in deception loses his ability to see moral issues as they really are. He becomes easily fooled because he is looking for anything that will justify his choice to disobey known truth.

The circle of deceiving and being deceived is difficult to break. It rarely ends and it often worsens. Even a discerning person can lose the facility to see clearly when he ignores deception in himself or others. The result of disregarding deception in others is that we can easily become compromisers ourselves. We adapt! This makes us vulnerable to the very sin that we excuse in others. Solomon wrote, "Acquitting the guilty and condemning the innocent—the LORD detests them both" (Proverbs 17:15).

The Art of Control

Manipulation means the "art of control." The person in deception tries to control others so they will act or react according to his wishes. He often uses unethical or immoral means of getting what he wants. He does not want others controlling him because this takes control out of his hands. He will go out of his way to avoid situations in which he does not have control.

Whenever we try to impose our will on others, it is easy to use partial truth—hiding the complete truth about something. Partial truth is a form of deception. Consider the pastor who tries to convince the church board to approve a new building while he secretly withholds vital financial information. It gets worse as the deceiver is successful in his manipulation. He may reason that he is "doing it for their own good." The pastor may rationalize, *They wouldn't understand the financial statement anyway.*

When we confront a manipulator, we can become the object of hostility or more manipulation. The manipulator may try to transfer guilt to control others.

A man I know carried on an affair with another woman for years before his wife learned of his escapades. At that point he decided to leave her and their two children and move in with his mistress. His wife was willing to reconcile the marriage, but she finally filed for divorce when the mistress became pregnant. One day, while he was visiting his children, he said to his ex-wife, "Since you don't want me around anymore, I've decided to get married." He was trying to justify his sinful actions in his mind by transferring the blame to her.

"It is a characteristic of those who are evil," writes Scott Peck, "to judge others as evil. Unable to acknowledge their own imperfection, they must explain away their flaws by blaming others."[3]

Impatience: Learning Not to Move

Those in deception are often impetuous and presumptuous, and their choices usually reflect these character flaws. When decisions turn sour, they search for justification. The Bible admonishes us, "Do not be anxious about anything, but in everything . . . present your requests to God" (Philippians 4:6). But an impatient person moves ahead of God without waiting for His guidance. When failure comes, he or she looks for a scapegoat.

King Saul's first error was to act hastily. He took matters into his own hands. He was unwilling to wait for Samuel to arrive before sacrificing the burnt offerings, so he did it himself. An impatient person is presumptuous and undisciplined. I have heard many Christians say, "There's no time to lose. God wants us to press on *now!*" Yet the Bible says, "With the Lord a day is like a thousand years, and a thousand years are like a day" (2 Peter 3:8). It is *we* who are in a hurry, not God. This does not mean that we should be inactive, ignoring the task of evangelization and growth. But part of our Christian lives is learning how to wait, and waiting is one thing few of us do well.

God understands our time limitations. When we act ahead of Him, we move out of His will and into our own.

Compartmentalization

It is easy in our society to live a duplicitous life. We can download pornography from our computers, for example, instead of going to the local adult bookstore to buy it. It has become easier for Christians to commit their personal sins anonymously.

It has also become simpler (for some of the reasons I have mentioned in this chapter) to lead a compartmentalized life. Such a life can be characterized by the statement "What I do in the sanctity of my home is nobody's business." We can engage in all sorts of sins without anyone ever knowing—sometimes not even those in our own households. This trend means moral Christians must further guard themselves from temptation. We must become voluntarily accountable to our spouses, our families, our churches, our Christian friends, even to ourselves. If we do not, we will live compartmentalized lives, dividing our faith from the secret sins we cherish in our hearts.

This is exactly what a person in self-deception does, hiding his immorality from outsiders. But genuine Christianity means we live the same way at home, or in the privacy of our own hearts, as we do on a business trip or anywhere else. Our awareness of the pitfalls will keep us free from the dangers of self-deception.

We will see in the next chapter that, just as there are personal traits or tendencies that develop in those who compromise moral truth, there are consequences—and these can be devastating.

Chapter Highlights

All people in self-deception display certain characteristics. Watch for these danger signs:

- A lack of genuine repentance followed by an external change in attitude and behavior.
- A form of narcissism characterized by redefining the absolute truth of the Bible to suit one's lifestyle or plans.
- An unwillingness to obey known truth. This is characterized by persistent sin, often excused on the basis of God's grace or mercy.
- A tendency to project sin onto others, particularly those who confront the person in self-deception.
- An inability to see the seriousness of sinful behavior, either to oneself or to one's family.

Black Holes
and Moral Tar Pits

The greatest danger we face in America is not that people don't believe in God, but they believe in God without allowing Him to rule their everyday affairs.

Floyd McClung

Woe to those who call evil good, and good evil; who substitute darkness for light and light for darkness.

Isaiah 5:20, NASB

Amy gave her heart to Christ when she was seven, but by the time she was 23, her life was a mess.

She had grown up in a warm and affectionate home. Her father was a successful businessman. Her mother was a prayer warrior. Amy attended church, sang in the choir and went to camp. She displayed no outward signs of rebellion. Yet before she left high school, she was abusing alcohol, drugs and sex. Amy would crawl out of her bedroom window and party, often until dawn. After a night of partying, her car would reek of the pungent mixture of vomit and alcohol. Her mother wept and prayed. She remembers thinking, the night the police brought Amy to the front door, *Is this really my daughter?*

At twenty Amy became pregnant. She went away to school, then put her baby up for adoption. Afterward Amy went to Bible school to make a fresh start. But Bible school was not the answer. Her family soon learned she was pregnant again, this time by a seventeen-year-old missions student!

I recall meeting with Amy along with several caring believers. We were unable to dissuade her from compounding her sin by entering into a disastrous marriage. Finally she told us, "It doesn't matter. I've already made up my mind."

Several years later, after physical and emotional abuse, the marriage fell apart. Amy is now a single mother struggling to make it from day to day.

God spoke through the prophet Isaiah concerning His people: "'The ox knows his master, the donkey his owner's manger, but Israel does not know, my people do not understand.' . . . They have forsaken the LORD . . . and turned their backs on him" (Isaiah 1:3–4). Amy's self-deception began as she turned away from the truth she knew and started forging her own path.

We become accustomed to, and eventually misled by, repetitive sin. When we continue in rebellion, it ends in spiritual death. M. Scott Peck writes that evil people "are men and women of obviously strong will, determined to have their own way." He adds, "We are not created evil or forced to be evil, but we become evil slowly over time through a long series of choices."[1] Although God's Word says that mankind has a propensity or leaning to do wrong, we are in no way compelled against our wills to do evil. The choices Peck refers to—or excuses for immorality— have progressive consequences for the Christian.

In this chapter we will explore the consequences of self-deception, discussing scriptural insights for each stage along the way.

Deception by Degree

Deception does not happen overnight. It may take years before the result catches up with us. The origin, however, is always the same: a single wrong choice. This choice begins a process that builds layer upon layer.

I have listed nine stages of this layering process as it proceeds from God's silence to His turning us over to our own immoral behavior.

- Divine silence (Psalm 66:18)
- Loss of discernment (Isaiah 29:14)
- Growing obscurity of truth and revelation (Romans 1:25)
- Inability to acknowledge the truth (2 Timothy 3:7)
- Deceiving and being deceived (2 Timothy 3:13)
- Desperation for acceptance (1 Samuel 15:30)
- A false sense of salvation (Matthew 7:21–23)
- Separation from God (Ephesians 4:18)
- Reprobate mind (Romans 1:28)

1. Divine Silence: Where Is God?

God often uses silence to get our attention. King David knew what it felt like to experience the silence of God. He knew the moment he began lusting after Bathsheba that it was wrong. He decided to indulge in his fantasies anyway. David's road to spiritual recovery was long and arduous. Although God forgave him, His forgiveness came *after* David repented of his sin.

Some people plan their sin secretly. They calculate their next act of rebellion with hardly a thought, and they fully accept the inevitability of a life filled with sin. But God says:

> *It is impossible for those who have once been enlightened,* who have tasted the heavenly gift, who have shared in the Holy Spirit, . . . if they fall away, *to be brought back to repen-*

tance, because to their loss they are crucifying the Son of God all over again and subjecting him to public disgrace.

Hebrews 6:4–6, emphasis added

God is trying to bridge the gap between Himself and His people. It is His desire to renew and restore. When we deliberately act contrary to His Word, we lose our communion with Him. But if we turn from our immorality, we can restore our right standing with Him.

Some churches are confused about how forgiveness works. It is, and always has been, two-way. God will extend His mercy and forgiveness when we stop living in disobedience. If there is any tenuousness to our salvation, it rests not with God's ability to keep us, nor does it consist of a singular act of sin. It lies exclusively with our unwillingness to forsake our wickedness and turn to Him with a whole heart. Think again of that man saying to his bride, "Honey, I really love you, but be patient with me. I've been seeing another woman for many years, and it will take some time to break off the relationship." Ridiculous!—yet this is the kind of foolishness some of us expect of God: the benefits of salvation without the accompanying fidelity.

Those who ignore God's Word or His ways *will* lose touch with Him. King David spent a year trying to reestablish the fellowship he lost with God before his sin. Those in self-deception may profess to be in right standing with God. But their hearts are far away and they lose their ability to hear from Him.

2. Loss of Discernment

The Pharisees were intelligent. They knew God's Word. They had daily access to it. Nevertheless, their hearts were hard. They became rigid and unbending. Their knowledge of God's Word was not enough to keep them free from deception. They had no discernment because they were unwilling to accept truth at any cost. Nor were they willing to see, accept and apply the truth of God's Word to their lives. They were afraid of change—of turning their intellectual knowledge into heart knowledge.

Some of us do not obey the knowledge we have. Intellectual enlightenment of any kind always carries with it responsibility. When we fail to give in to the pleading of the Holy Spirit, we lose our ability to "correctly [handle] the word of truth" (2 Timothy 2:15).

We cannot compartmentalize our spiritual lives. A disregard for truth in any area creates a climate ripe for individual or corporate apostasy. It leads to spiritual blindness. Jesus spoke of this blindness when He said, "While seeing, they may see and not perceive; and while hearing, they may hear and not understand . . ." (Mark 4:12, NASB). The person in deception loses his ability to discern because he has compromised truth in some area of life.

3. Obscurity of Truth

The person who lacks moral discernment also has difficulty perceiving moral truth. In a spiritual sense, all compromise leads to an obscuring of truth and revelation. Those who "[exchange] the truth of God for a lie" (Romans 1:25) have trouble differentiating between truth and error. The only way to prevent this is to stay on track, guarding the truth of God's Word within our own hearts.

Years ago I was climbing the North Palisade, a steep granite pinnacle in the Sierra Nevada mountain range of California. After completing the 14,000-foot ascent, I began to make my way back down. But on the summit I became disoriented and began to descend the western slope instead of the eastern. Soon I knew I was heading in the wrong direction but I did not change course. As darkness fell on the craggy granite cliffs around me, I began to panic. If I had stopped long enough to retrace my steps, I would not have strayed so far off-course. My choices led to an uncomfortable bivouac under the stars!

The way to stay on course spiritually is to gird ourselves with God's Word. The word *gird* means *to surround or bind.* There are times we need to check our course before going further. Are we heading in the right direction? Many of us keep going when we should stop and check our moral compass. To keep us on track, God has equipped us with His Word. It is, as King David said, "a lamp to my feet and a light for my path" (Psalm 119:105). When we refuse the power of the Gospel in our life, we begin to obscure the truth.

4. Being Closed to Truth

A disciple of Christ is, by nature, a seeker of truth. Even if he or she is in error, confrontation should lead this disciple back onto the right path. If another climber had come along during my climb in the Sierras and said, "Hey, you're on the wrong course," I would have asked for help. But as deception worsens, we close ourselves off to truth. This is the first in a series of debilitating results that start a *hardening of heart.* Dietrich Bonhoeffer wrote about this gradual hardening:

> At first [the disobedient person] was aware enough of his disobedience. With his increasing hardness of heart, that awareness grows even fainter, and in the end he becomes so enmeshed that he loses all capacity for hearing the word, and faith is quite impossible.[2]

Paul wrote that in latter times men "will turn their ears away from the truth" (2 Timothy 4:4). The prophet Daniel understood the danger of ignoring truth. He wrote, "We have not sought the favor of the LORD our God by turning from our sins and giving attention to your truth" (Daniel 9:13).

The Bible makes it clear who will be most susceptible to apostasy: those who "[refuse] to love the truth and so be saved. . . . [They] have not believed the truth but have delighted in wickedness" (2 Thessalonians 2:10, 12).

Being closed to truth no longer manifests itself in isolated occurrences of disobedience. It reveals itself by rewriting biblical truth and compromising in both big and little ways. We use company phones because "we work hard." We lie because "we don't want to hurt someone's feelings." By compromising in small things, we open the floodgates for compromise in larger areas. We must not accept such excuses in ourselves or others.

The prophet Isaiah could have been speaking directly to our generation when he wrote, "These are rebellious people, deceitful children, children unwilling to listen to the LORD's instruction. They say to the seers . . . 'Tell us pleasant things, prophesy illusions. . . . Stop confronting us with the Holy One of Israel!'" (Isaiah 30:9–11). Those in deception do not really *want* to hear the truth. It makes them uncomfortable. Like the witnesses to the stoning of Stephen, they cover their ears and insult the one who declares the truth.

When the truth of God's Word penetrates our hearts, it produces one of two responses. The first is an immediate desire to obey or get back on the right track. The second is to develop excuses for not responding as we should. This yields spiritual separation—and ultimately death.

We cannot afford to lose our hunger for the truth of God's Word. Otherwise we shut ourselves off to further growth and invite spiritual stagnation. It is not enough to know Scripture. Satan knows it well and uses it for his own ends, as he proved while tempting Jesus in the wilderness. The key is to take the truth of God's Word and make personal application.

5. Deception Breeds Deception

The harsh words Jesus spoke to the Pharisees were designed as a wake-up call on their misplaced priorities. His reproofs may have had little to do with trying to change them and more to do with warning those who revered these pretenders. The religious leaders of Jesus' time did not represent God faithfully and were dragging others down with them.

In the later stages, those in deception believe they are right and all others wrong. When confronted, they become defensive and resistant. They try to convince themselves of the correctness of their position. In such a state, they easily persuade others. This is a picture of the Pharisees.

Power is the potential to influence. Jesus was dismantling the props the Pharisees used to verify their godliness, stripping them of their excuses, laying bare their religious hypocrisy. When a "renegade" Jesus brought truth out in the open, the people were able to make their own decisions.

We have present-day illusions, too. These enable us or others to proclaim our own innocence against the truth of God's Word. It was in responding to just such a situation that God sent Gideon to tear down the altar to Baal. Only by tearing down the existing altar could Gideon build a proper altar to the Lord.

We must shatter the notion that we can base our Christianity on passive acceptance of carnality. God wants us to remove the Baals from our own lives, too. When we leave them intact, we cannot give full allegiance to Him, nor can we receive the blessings He desires for us. If we fail to act aggressively when dealing with deception, we will unintentionally give birth to illegitimate spiritual offspring. This produces believers who are vulnerable to the world and impotent in the Church.

6. Yearning for Acceptance

After God rejected Saul from being king over Israel, Saul said to Samuel, "Please honor me before the elders of my people and before Israel; come back with me, so that I may worship the LORD *your* God" (1 Samuel 15:30, emphasis added). Saul cared less about worshiping God than about how he looked in other people's eyes. In fact, his act of worship became a means to his own exaltation.

Our desperation for external acceptance is no different from what it was more than 2,500 years ago during the time of Ezekiel: "They sit before you as My people, but they do the lustful desires expressed by their mouth, and their heart goes after their gain. . . . For *they hear your words, but they do not practice them*" (Ezekiel 33:31–32, NASB, emphasis added).

When we lack discernment, this outward sign of spirituality can confuse us. We may hear someone rattle off Scriptures or offer eloquent prayers, but these are not the signs of a genuinely moral life. In fact, those in self-deception can benefit in an unexpected way from association with the Church. Since biblical obedience is not essential to membership in many churches, the Body of Christ may provide the acceptance those in deception (like Saul) hunger for, and help them maintain an external posture of godliness.

This does not mean we refuse people who come from a sinful past. Nor does it mean we reject people who are imperfect. We must not tolerate or accept as normal, however, behavior that violates the moral teaching of the Bible. To do otherwise is not to communicate our compassion for the lost but, whether we mean to or not, to convey our disdain for God. Some of our churches even encourage a "form of godliness" (as we saw in the last chapter) while "denying its power" (2 Timothy 3:5). We demand little in the way of spiritual maturity because it thrills us to have people sitting in our pews. As a result, we accept or actually create "fractional" Christianity—a faith in only those tenets of Christ's teachings that are comfortable for us personally.

One of the reasons people are desperate for acceptance is that their self-esteem is tied not to who they are in Christ but to how well they look or perform. The true path to freedom, by contrast, comes through denying self. And when we crave the acceptance of others more than we enjoy the pleasure of God, we become more willing to compromise.

7. A False Sense of Security

The most serious results of deception are the last three: surrendering one's salvation, being separated from God and a reprobate state. Each of these conditions represents a gradual severing of a once-fruitful relationship with God. In each case the individual selects his or her own fate. God, who does everything possible to draw us to Himself, finally says, "Enough!" and turns the person over to his or her own desires.

Jesus' stunning words in Matthew are a warning to anyone who equates works with spiritual fruit: "Not everyone who says to me, 'Lord, Lord,' will enter the kingdom of heaven, but only he who does the will of my Father who is in heaven" (Matthew 7:21). George Otis Jr. writes that such people "are extremely harmful because they present a warped and incomplete rendering of the nature and character of God to the world."[3]

Some people believe that action or accomplishment must be related to godliness, and that no matter what we do, even reject God's Word, our salvation will remain intact. It sounds comforting. Indeed, the initial decision for salvation is a matter of individual choice. But this teaching is detrimental to spiritual growth and maturity because it lulls many believers into a false sense of certainty and produces spiritual malaise. The issue has nothing to do with the traditional debate between works and grace. The question is simply one of choice. God does not compel us to keep our commitment to Him. Our obedience is evidence of our relationship to Christ, just as fidelity in marriage signifies commitment to one's spouse. Our outward behavior is a manifestation of our love for God.

The Word says, "We know that we have come to know him if we obey his commands. The man who says, 'I know him,' but does not do what he commands is a liar" (1 John 2:3–4). Jesus made it clear that if we love Him, we will obey His commands. The biblical correlation between our faith and our behavior is inseparable. And our morality must hinge on two things: our faith in God's Word and on behavior that emanates from our beliefs. Jesus said that a disciple "must deny himself and take up his cross daily" (Luke 9:23). Paul wrote, "I die every day—I mean that, brothers" (1 Corinthians 15:31). Behind these injunctions is a warning that a constant struggle is taking place. This battle requires that we always be on the alert lest we get off-track spiritually.

The person in deception identifies with doctrinal positions that reinforce the spiritual security of the believer apart from any outward manifestation of godliness, without any change in thinking or lifestyle. And a person's belief in such a doctrine does little to dissuade him or her from further rebellion.

8. Separation from God

All sin separates man and his Creator. So what makes the sin of deception different from any other sin? One important distinction. Deception is not the result of one or two sinful actions; it is the habitual rejection of truth. When we are in deception, we may be unaware of our separation from God. We are like a driver headed in the wrong direction without knowing it. And, tragically, if we do not know we are on the wrong road, we will not take corrective action to get back where we ought to be.

When we deal with our sin properly, it repairs the breach in our relationship with God and gets us back on track. But those in deception often argue, "God accepts me as I am. He knows I'm not perfect." What they are saying is, "I'm perfectly happy with the path I'm on." These excuses make it easier for them to accept their behavior as a matter of routine.

Isaiah gave a strong warning to God's people: "Your iniquities have separated you from your God; your sins have hidden his face from you, so that he will not hear" (Isaiah 59:2). When we try to cover our sin, it leads to further deception. And when we refuse to deal with immorality in our lives, eventually God turns His face from us. Paul offered the following description of idolatrous Gentiles:

> Darkened in their understanding [lack of discernment], excluded from the life of God [no salvation], because of the ignorance that is in them [closed to truth], because of the hardness of their heart [rebellion]; and they, having become callous [reprobate], have given themselves over to sensuality, for the practice of every kind of impurity with greediness.
>
> Ephesians 4:18–19, NASB

It is the *practice* of disobedience that leads to self-deception. When we proclaim allegiance to Christ, we cannot walk in rebellion and take comfort in the appurtenances of the faith.

9. Reprobate Mind: Choosing Our Way

The word *reprobate* means *rejected* or *abandoned*. We find it in its singular form just three times in the New Testament. The Bible uses the word *depraved* interchangeably with *reprobate*. Paul wrote, "Since they did not think it worthwhile to retain the knowledge of God, he gave them over to a depraved mind, to do what ought not to be done" (Romans 1:28). These individuals had, at some time, recognized and served God, as the word *retain* indicates. One reason God turned them over to their lusts was that they had begun to infect and mislead others: "Although they know God's righteous decree that those who do such things deserve death, they not only continue to do these very things but also approve of those who practice them" (verse 32).

The reprobate are often unaware of their disobedience and "suppress the truth by their wickedness. . . . Although they claimed to be wise, they became fools . . . [and] exchanged the truth of God for a lie" (verses 18, 22, 25).

Jeremiah wrote about the people of God who "[turn] away in continual apostasy. . . . They hold fast to deceit, they refuse to return. . . . No man repented of his wickedness . . . they have rejected the word of the LORD" (Jeremiah 8:5, 6, 9, NASB). Isaiah wrote that God "has smeared over their eyes so that they cannot see and their hearts so that they cannot comprehend. . . . A deceived heart has turned [them] aside" (Isaiah 44:18, 20, NASB).

Perhaps the most solemn rebuke comes from Hosea:

"Their deeds do not permit them to return to their God. A spirit of prostitution is in their heart; they do not acknowledge the LORD. . . . When they go . . . to seek the LORD, they will not find him; *he has withdrawn himself from them.*"
Hosea 5:4, 6, emphasis added

With sin God has His limits. The perversion in Sodom is a classic example. We saw in chapter 4 that while Lot entertained angelic guests sent from God, the Sodomites demanded to have intercourse with them. God said, "Enough!" Because of His love for Lot and His hatred for their sin, God intervened to blind the Sodomites and eventually destroy their city.

God does everything possible to draw us to Himself without overriding our wills. Yet when we persist against the nudging of the Holy Spirit, He will not interfere with our choices. When we persevere in rebellion, God eventually turns us over to our lusts. In Sodom and Rome, the sin was sexual depravity. But we can sever our relationship with God through indulgence in other sins, too. Paul lists *greed, slander, idolatry, adultery, theft, swindling* and *drunkenness* as sins that can keep us out of the Kingdom of God if we allow them to become a way of life (see 1 Corinthians 6:9–10). But in writing to the believers in Corinth, Paul adds the past tense emphasis: "And that is what some of you *were*" (verse 11, emphasis added).

Corporate Effects: No Victimless Sin

Now that we have studied the nine stages of the "layering process" of self-deception, let's raise another question: Are there consequences of so-called "victimless" crime? This is crime that ostensibly affects only the individual, and includes homosexuality, prostitution, suicide and drug addiction. Our society considers these forms of deviance less serious. Are they?

Some say, "Sexual behavior between consenting adults is a private matter and no one's business." But with hundreds of thousands dead from AIDS and others dying daily, can we still adopt this *laissez faire* attitude? Isn't the expense for life insurance, medical care and research our business? Who should be responsible for these costs? The disease is spreading rapidly, despite our efforts to educate or hand out condoms.

There are always at least two victims when we sin: ourselves and God. More often it involves others as well. Let's look briefly at one other example: divorce.

Peter Nickerson, economics professor at Seattle University, puts the cost of divorce in perspective. "The taxpayers pay a tremendous burden," he says. "In this state more than half a billion dollars are paid out in AFDC [Aid to Families with Dependent Children] payments, and as much as half of that may be going to children of divorce. And that doesn't include the fact that the schools are so screwed up—kids there are hungry or ornery and their parents are fighting."[4]

We affect the lives of our children through divorce. We pay a higher price for retail items because of theft. Our insurance rates increase because of drunk drivers. We suffer serious emotional damage from abortion. The results of such permissive laws weaken the social fabric of our culture through a diminishing respect for life.

Let's look at the consequences of self-deception on people outside and inside the Kingdom of God.

Leading Unbelievers in Rebellion

I tuned in to a radio talk show discussion on the subject of evil one afternoon. The secular panel made broad and dogmatic statements about the immorality of the Holocaust—statements with which I agreed. Yet on what underlying premise, I wondered, had the panelists come to these conclusions? If I were to disagree, would they try to force the same "narrow-minded absolutism" on me that I as a born-again Christian am often accused of trying to foist on them? The discussion left me wondering what the basis of secular man's morality is.

For the Christian, as we have seen, God's Word serves as the absolute basis of truth. Our morality comes from a source higher than ourselves and reflects the transcendence of God's immutable character. By failing to accept this reality, we drift aimlessly in a sea of subjectivism and emotion. On issues important to the unbeliever—like the evil that was the Holocaust—he or she argues with passion. But on *any* issue, arguments are hollow when there is no absolute truth to transcend experience or opinion. Every point of view is equally valid.

Even Christians get caught up in subjectivity when they give in persistently to the flesh. This leads easily to self-deception. And when we ignore God's Word, it has an unmistakable influence on unbelievers in the world.

God, who wants His people to serve as a light to the world, speaks harshly about those who lead others in rebellion. He calls them "false sons, sons who refuse to listen" (Isaiah 30:9, NASB). God accompanied the plagues on Egypt with statements like this: "So that you will know that I, the LORD, am in this land" (Exodus 8:22). He added, "I will make a distinction between my people and your people" (verse 23). God clearly recognizes the pull of the world. But when we fill our life with excuses for misbehavior, unbelievers see little difference between their actions and those of professing Christians, and scoff at God. They reason that we serve a God who is powerless, and we prove them right by the way we live.

A popular Christian bumper sticker typifies the dilemma: *Christians aren't perfect, just forgiven.* While clinging to such slogans may be theologically correct and serves to ease our collective conscience, it reduces the vitality of the Gospel. In truth, such a philosophy provides fuel for our already burgeoning supply of excuses to live carnal lives.

But if we live the same as our worldly neighbors, how can we honestly convince them of the life-changing power of the Gospel? We *are* the Gospel message! When we fail to yield our life to its truth, we compromise it. When we respond out of selfish motives, our choices can actually steer unbelievers away from God, rather than into His loving arms.

Licensing Immorality in the Church

Self-deception also has an incapacitating effect on the Church. By refusing to end obvious sin, we unintentionally encourage it. This produces a scattering effect that weakens the Church, like planting weeds in a beautiful garden.

The call for holiness throughout Scripture is a call for separation from all that is worldly and profane. Sanctification—being set apart for God—is a call to forsake whatever draws us away from, rather than toward, the living God. "A little leaven," wrote Paul, "leaveneth the whole lump" (Galatians 5:9, KJV). When we permit "little" sins in our own lives or in the corporate Body, they slowly choke our own vitality.

Our tolerance for rebellion also gives license to other believers. Those who practice deception breed new followers—missionaries of the gospel of self. Any form of moral permissiveness gradually suffocates the life of the Church. Before long God's values are no longer relevant. An Episcopal rector discussing morality reflected this problem: "We change interpretations as each new era brings new insights into human behavior." And a parishioner commented, "No one has a right to say how people can be happy. The church has to loosen its reins a bit. We have a changing world here, and we have to open our doors and encourage people to have loving relationships no matter who they're with."[5]

Why would the Church have to loosen its reins? For one simple reason: to accommodate people who do not want to come under the Lordship of Jesus Christ.

But if the Church does not take a stand for biblical morality, we will find ourselves submerged in the moral filth of each passing era. A relativistic, ever-changing system of morality has nothing to do with biblical truth. In fact, it runs contrary to sound doctrine. Morality is not part of an evolutionary process. Our Creator has not changed His mind, nor has human nature changed. And there is no place for "progressive moral enlightenment." When we license immorality, even tacitly, we leave the gate to the spiritual henhouse open to the wolves.

The Consequences of Personal Influence

In a study made famous in the 1950s, social psychologist Solomon Asch studied the effects of conformity. What, he wondered, would individuals do when faced with the pressure to conform to the consensus of a group? Here is how Asch's research worked.

A group of seven people arrived for the experiment, six of them secret confederates of the researcher, only one actually being tested. The experimenter presented a card with a straight twelve-inch line. Then he showed them three additional cards labeled *A*, *B* and *C*. These contained lines six, twelve and eighteen inches in length. The difference in the lengths of the lines was obvious. The experimenter asked the participants to compare the other three lines and determine the closest match. Since the person being tested was one of the last in the group to answer, he was forced to sit through incorrect answers from every participant who preceded him. He was placed in a dilemma: to remain independent of the group and respond according to what his eyes told him, or go along with the group and conform to the majority.

One out of three individuals caught between countervailing forces, Asch found, abandoned the evidence of his or her senses and yielded to group pressure to conform.

About a dozen years ago, perhaps unwisely, I duplicated the Asch study in a church high school group. My version of Asch's research caused quite a stir among the teenagers I tested. One obviously distraught girl was humiliated, and I regretted what could be construed as a deceptive way to find out which Christian teens were most susceptible to peer pressure. But I found the numbers roughly the same as Asch had for the youngsters I studied—approximately one-third of the group.

There are many reasons for Christians to conform. Some of us wish to avoid the stigma of negative labels like *fun-*

damentalist or *narrow-minded.* Others are reluctant to lose face in front of others. In any case, the desire to reduce embarrassment leads approximately one in three to deny the reality of his or her senses or beliefs. Asch concluded that "we follow the advice or copy the behavior of others because we feel they have knowledge or information that will be helpful to us."[6]

In a variation of the study, Asch found two influential factors that lead to conformity: *group unanimity* and *status.*

Group Unanimity

First, regarding group unanimity, it takes just one other person in a group to stand up for what his senses reveal to prevent others from falling prey to the group.

It is difficult to be a dissenter when someone in deception is working hard to achieve harmony among those closest to him—his family, friends or employees. The person in deception often works especially hard to influence the conduct or thinking of those around him. A Christian in deception will use manipulation, deceit, threats, even Scripture to change how others think. You may live or work with such a person. You may even see yourself in this description. A dissenter (as we will see later) may be the one object standing between a person and his or her immoral conduct. Standing alone against group consensus is never easy but it is sometimes necessary.

There are two equally important lessons to draw from this point. First, as Christians we must stand unashamedly for moral truth. If we champion God's Word, our posture will influence other (perhaps weaker) believers. Second, it takes only a single dissenter to break the influence others can have on us.

The inverse is also true. What happens when an individual encourages someone in self-deception? Only a little urging is needed to affirm individuals in illicit behavior and self-deception. When they receive it, they can harm other Christians in turn by encouraging ungodly behavior, driving them as well into self-deception.

Carl, who has been in Christian leadership since the mid-1970s, found himself in serious trouble in his church. His life and ministry were in a state of disaster due to a series of wrong moral choices. Some of his staff members sought help from his ministry elders, who wisely put Carl on a leave of absence. During that time he was under the care of godly men whose ministry to his mental and spiritual condition could have made an immense difference in his life.

Nevertheless, a young couple on staff at the church were unhappy with the structure imposed by the board. They felt it was their duty to intervene in the healing process of their spiritually ailing leader. So, week in and week out, this couple undermined the work of Carl's counselors, the ministry board and the Holy Spirit. There is no question in my mind that this couple believed they were doing what was right. They felt they were being loyal. But almost singlehandedly they could have blocked this man's spiritual and moral recovery.

Our desire to show compassion can actually encourage further sinful behavior. When this happens, we are interfering with the work of the Holy Spirit in someone else's life under the guise of mercy or love. Often this is all it takes for the person in deception to become further entrenched in his or her sin.

Status

The second influential factor in Asch's study leading to conformity is status. The revered status of the Pharisees, who offered a false representation of God, made it difficult for the common people to gain an authentic view of Him. The result: paralysis in the people's pursuit of truth.

When we build a relationship exclusively on individual need, acceptance or interdependence, it can be mutually destructive. The young couple in the church probably felt insecure without their leader. But, like King Saul, they took important spiritual matters into their own hands. Their pastor needed their support and they complied. But to ignore sinful behavior for the sake of preserving the relationship or status quo is a tacit endorsement of disobedience. Mutual acceptance regardless of behavior is the glue of dysfunctional relationships. When there is no room for pointing out error, just acceptance of one another without condition, "positive-only" friendships often expand into cliques, clubs or prayer groups in which the unwritten maxim blocks truth and morality.

From such relationships we must flee. When we stop facing sinful conduct in one another, we become vulnerable to ungodly persuasion in our life. We must hold to the values that Calvary reinforced two thousand years ago.

In the previous chapters we have encountered again and again the role of human will in the development of self-deception. It is always the human will acting to fulfill its own desires that leads a person into morally deceptive actions or habits. Spiritually speaking, however, human beings are not alone on this planet. God's Word makes it clear that we have an adversary plotting and exploiting every opportunity to bring us down. This has been Satan's intent from the Garden of Eden. How exactly does he influence our moral behavior? This is the subject of the following chapter.

Chapter Highlights

- The results of self-deception are progressive. When we fail to deal with sin, it becomes more acute.

- God never overrides the will in our decisions to accept or reject Him. And our choices to do His will verify the authenticity of our faith.
- The way to stay on course is to gird our minds with the Word of God. Many of us keep going when we should stop and check our spiritual compass.
- Knowing God's Word is not enough. We must apply the truth of His Word to our every action.
- Our choices influence ourselves and those around us. Can you identify ways your past choices have affected others?
- Are you facilitating anyone who is not walking according to God's Word? A support network of any kind will keep a person in deception from breaking free from his or her sin.

The Father of Lies

It does not matter how small the sins are, provided
that their cumulative effect is to edge the man away
from the light and out into the nothing . . . indeed,
the safest road to hell is the gradual one.

The Screwtape Letters, C. S. Lewis

The only power that Satan has is through human
belief in its lies.

M. Scott Peck

The most effective weapon our adversary has against
the Church is the distortion of truth. We recognize Satan,
and rightly so, as the liar and destroyer that he is. Yet without the ability to blend truth and error, his work would be
much more difficult. It is through his garbling of truth that
many believers become confused. We need only look to
the wilderness temptation to see how Satan misused Scripture to bait the Lord. Jessie Penn-Lewis wrote, "The devil
mixes his lies with the truth, for he must use truth to carry
his lies."[1]

In this chapter we will look at how Satan affects our
lives. We will examine the balance between individual freedom and satanic influence. Some churches today tend to
blame the devil for almost everything. Others swing too

141

far in the other direction, excluding the possibility of satanic interference at all. If you have committed your life to Christ, you may doubt that Satan is able to deceive you to any degree, or you may assume you are immune from his influence. Finally we want to examine *how* Satan influences us—a question that has no simple answer, since he blinds people and cultures in a variety of ways.

What Is Evil?

Do you know what evil looks like? In an age of moral uncertainty, who has the right to determine what is or is not evil? Like deception, evil is as amorphous as it is insidious. An abortion protester places his body across the entrance to a family planning clinic. To him, anyone picketing for reproductive rights and women's choice is evil. Then there is the social worker making rounds in the inner city who finds it difficult to do the job. Husbands batter wives. Adolescents feel the tug to join the local gang. Old and young alike fall prey to roving thugs. Children suffer. The system seems evil because people are poor and helpless.

Most people would call Hitler, Stalin and Pol Pot evil. We agree that Charles Manson and Jeffrey Dahmer were either mentally ill or demon-possessed—probably both. We concur that the masterminds behind the terrorist attacks in Algeria, Bosnia or Chechnya are evil. Yet the designation of *evil* is more difficult to apply to self or family. And the closer we get to evil, the less we can see it. Just ask the Germans who lived around Dachau or Buchenwald concentration camps during the Second World War.

It is ironic that truth can be spoken by those who are evil. We see good in an evil person and it confuses us. Some of Hitler's top officers were known to be affectionate husbands and loving fathers.

An essay in *Time* defines evil as "the bad hardened into the absolute."[2] Does this mean we can be bad some of the time and still not be evil? By what standard do we define *bad*? The Old Testament defines it as abandoning God or violating His commands or covenant. In essence, evil is rejecting God as the Ruler of our lives. If there is a difference between sin and evil, it lies in our unwillingness to acknowledge wrongdoing or deal with it.

One of Satan's schemes is to eradicate the notion of evil in many people's minds without removing its effects. When Satan cannot remove the notion of evil, he defines it only in its most extreme form. This serves to remove any possibility of our own evil. It is always something "out there"—beyond us. Satan's strategy is to provide us with the worst cases, thereby reducing our willingness to see our own guilt.

Who Is Satan?

Before we examine Satan's strategies, let's take a look at some of his attributes. These may alter your perception of him. Satan is beautiful (Ezekiel 28:12), proud (Ezekiel 28:17) and deceitful (Revelation 12:9). He has memory (Matthew 4:6), power (Revelation 2:10) and intelligence (2 Corinthians 2:11). Like all created beings, he has a will (2 Timothy 2:26). He has organizational ability (1 Timothy 4:1), plans and desires (Luke 22:31) and the ability to get angry (Revelation 12:12). The Bible lists 22 distinct and descriptive names for him. The most notable—*Satan*—appears 52 times in Scripture. His name means *Adversary*.

Satan is active, offensive and tireless. Like God, he has a throne and a kingdom. He has worshipers, ministers and angels to carry out his work. He fellowships with them. He tempts humans, performs miracles, perverts the truth, blinds human beings to truth, instigates false doctrine, afflicts and accuses.

Diablos: *The Accuser*

In Greek, *devil* or *diablos* means *accuser.* We know Satan as "the accuser of our brethren" (Revelation 12:10, KJV). But in self-deception we see the opposite trait: Satan is the empathizer. He provides comfort to those whom the Holy Spirit convicts. In short, he will do anything he can to interfere with the work of God. He did so in the Garden of Eden. He will do it in your life and mine.

The northern Greek town of Philippi was the staging ground for such interference and a bizarre confrontation between good and evil. Soon after the apostle Paul and his associate Silas arrived in the Roman port after a long voyage, a young woman met them. She told fortunes for a living. Day after day she followed them, shouting, "These men are servants of the Most High God, who are telling you the way to be saved" (Acts 16:17). She spoke the truth. But when Paul and Silas were about to pray, the evil spirit controlling her did everything in its power to disrupt the work of the Lord. This led to a confrontation with the town magistrates, and Paul and Silas were beaten and thrown into prison. God's work could not be stopped, however, and that night He freed them and used them to convert their jailer and his family.

Even when truth is spoken, Satan betrays himself through disrupting the natural flow and purposes of God. The only way someone in Philippi could have recognized the evil spirit in the young woman was through its disruption of God's work. Today most believers would be unable to recognize such illusive tactics.

Satan also tries to disrupt the prayers of God's people. The prophet Daniel learned of Satan's power to interfere with God's plans. The angel of God [a demon could not have resisted the Son of God, nor would Jesus have needed the help of the archangel Michael] said to him in a vision, "Since the first day that you set your mind to gain understanding and to humble yourself before your God, your words were heard, and I have come in response to them. But the prince of the Persian kingdom resisted me twenty-one days" (Daniel 10:12–13).

If the prayers of godly men and women are ineffective, why would Satan try to stop them?

The Father of Lies

Satan has been a skillful manipulator, the grand master of deception, since the Garden of Eden. Jesus said, "He was a murderer from the beginning, not holding to the truth, for there is no truth in him. When he lies, he speaks his native language, for he is a liar and the father of lies" (John 8:44).

Satan must borrow truth to accomplish his purposes. He also uses diversions within our culture to interfere with what God wants to do. Do you see the devil's hand in secularism or materialism as much as in Communism or Hinduism? Do you recognize these as the crippling gods of a sadistic manipulator?

Herbert Schlossberg writes,

> Western society, in turning away from the Christian faith, has turned to other things. This process is commonly called secularization, [but that conveys] only the negative aspect. The word connotes the turning away from worship of God while ignoring that something is being turned to in its place.[3]

We are turning to all kinds of amusements to satisfy a soul that cannot rightly be satisfied by anything but God. These diversions are exactly what Satan wants. He uses them to keep us preoccupied so we will be of no use to God's Kingdom.

While many of us wallow in the inevitability of Satan's defeat, we forget that he is not defeated yet. And we assume, perhaps wrongly, that he accepts the certainty of his fate.

But could it be that our enemy expects to win the final battle? Certainly he knows Scripture. Even so, we know that he did not recognize the significance of Christ's death until it was accomplished (see 1 Corinthians 2:8). Perhaps he actually believes he can change future events in his favor.

Whatever the case, Satan is enormously powerful and immensely successful.

Strategy of Deceit

The first time we learn about Satan is in Genesis 3:1, where he is called *crafty*. He reappears throughout the Bible, from beginning to end, trying to thwart the work of God—appearing at last in Revelation as "the serpent of old who is called the devil and Satan, who deceives the whole world" (Revelation 12:9, NASB).

He does not act capriciously. In Eden he used the truth of God's command—"Did God really say, 'You must not eat from any tree in the garden'?" (Genesis 3:1)—to set up his own lie. He said, "You will not surely die. . . . For God knows that when you eat of it your eyes will be opened, and you will be like God, knowing good and evil" (verses 4–5).

The first element of Satan's deception, then, is to plant seeds of doubt in the mind of a believer about the absoluteness of God's Word. By producing doubt, Satan tries to discredit God. Any individual, church, book or thought that creates doubt about God's Word is satanic in origin (although this is not to say that anyone used by Satan is evil simply because he or she gets caught in his trap).

We can trace the second part of Satan's deception back to his pride. He proves his rebelliousness by countermanding God's Word, and he is clever enough to replace it with his own false statement. By doing so he calls into question the very morality of God! Did God lie? This is the implication he offers Eve: "You cannot trust God. His word is invalid."

The final part of Satan's strategy is found in this statement: "Your eyes will be opened" (verse 5). There is partial truth here. Indeed, Eve *could* see good and evil after she sinned. But Satan did not tell her the result of her disobedience.

Satan has always tried to package sin attractively. There is no better example than how he presents sexual lust. He cloaks it as love, never revealing the emotional or physical results.

Solomon prefaces his comment about the harlot by saying, "Treasure my commandments within you" (Proverbs 7:1, NASB). Then, in his descriptive commentary, Solomon puts these words into the harlot's mouth: "I have covered my bed with colored linens from Egypt. I have perfumed my bed with myrrh, aloes and cinnamon. . . . Let's enjoy ourselves with love!" (verses 16–18). But the youth who follows the harlot little knows "it will cost him his life. . . . Her house is a highway to the grave" (verses 23, 27).

The manipulation of our senses is part of Satan's strategy—the lust of the flesh and eyes. Eve's deception also began with what was "pleasing to the eye" (Genesis 3:6). The devil weaves into our thinking the fallacy that our senses deserve gratification. Jessie Penn-Lewis writes:

> The working upon the senses in the religious realm has long been Satan's special mode of deceiving men throughout the whole world. He knows how to soothe, and move, and work upon the senses in every possible way.[4]

Satan was successful in getting Eve's eyes off of God and the authority of His command. She gave in to illegitimate sensual fulfillment. Perhaps she reasoned, *Didn't God create this garden for my happiness? Why would He want to inhibit me?*

The deceptiveness of sin lies in our definition of *good*. We equate good with productivity, usefulness or pleasure.

The immediacy of our gratification supersedes the absoluteness of following God's will. Thus we, like Eve, fail to foresee the results that our rebellion will bear.

C. S. Lewis uncovered Satan's tactics as master deceiver through Uncle Wormwood's advice to his apprentice: "We do want, and we want very much, to make men treat Christianity as a means; preferably, of course, as a means to their own advancement, but failing that, as a means to anything."[5]

There is one final and perhaps most important word about Satan's strategy. We must recognize that we are all susceptible to his deception. All of us. In fact, the realization that we are vulnerable keeps us open to the truth of God. We cannot reason that we are immune to Satan's ways because we are or have been faithful to the Lord. Up until the point of her deception, Eve was also faithful. Nor does simply knowing God's Word protect us. It is only through the application of biblical knowledge that we can protect ourselves from Satan's deceiving ways.

Openings for Destruction

How much influence does Satan have in our lives? How was he able to deceive man? The answers to these questions come from opposite directions.

One proposition is that Satan has no influence over the life of a believer. The second is that Satan can cause a believer to sin. Does he?

Choosing to Sin

God made Himself vulnerable to hurt and rejection by creating man in His own image—with the ability to create. When we try to explain the existence of evil, it must be within the context of the freedom God created us to exercise. In his book *Spiritual Warfare for Every Believer* Dean Sherman writes, "Free will is more valuable than the absence of evil."[6] Sherman reasons that freedom to choose to return love, or not to return it, is the basis for relationship. God does not force us into an intimate relationship with Himself; He wants to *love* us into it. Human free will is mentioned or alluded to more than two thousand times in the Scriptures, and the phrase *whosoever will* appears 179 times.

The implication of moral freedom is that we are the originators of our actions. We alone are responsible for our choices. This is not to diminish the role that our environment has on us, nor does it ignore the influence the enemy has. Neither of these factors, however, *causes* us to sin. Adam and Eve were morally free to choose to obey God. They chose not to. The nature of freedom presupposes that our actions are without antecedent knowledge or causes.

The Bible tells us that God does not want "anyone to perish, but everyone to come to repentance" (2 Peter 3:9). We know, however, that all are not coming to repentance, and the reason is plain: "It is because they have forsaken my law, which I set before them; they have not obeyed me or followed my law. Instead, they have followed the stubbornness of their hearts . . ." (Jeremiah 9:13–14). It is clear in Scripture that human beings are guilty for their sin, and that they can assuage that guilt only though the redemptive power of Jesus Christ.

Leaving Places Untended

The Bible likens Satan to a robber and thief. The extent to which a thief can relieve us of our earthly possessions depends on how well we are protected. Similarly, if we leave certain areas of our lives unattended, we become vulnerable to moral failure. If you leave the door to your home open and a thief steals from you, should you be surprised?

There are at least two places Satan tries to invade. The first is *areas of moral flabbiness that we have not fully yielded to the Lord.* The easiest way for a thief to penetrate a home, as you know, is through an open door or window.

We are also vulnerable in *areas we leave unprotected.* A home with small children and an unfenced swimming pool is such an area. In our spiritual lives, unprotected areas are those we ignore—perhaps because we have never been attacked in these areas before. Gordon MacDonald writes, "An unguarded strength is a double weakness."[7] We may neglect marriage, family or fellowship, and suddenly find we are in trouble. Few of us plan for moral failure, and most will say it happened suddenly. But this is not true. The seeds of sin germinate in conditions conducive to their growth.

Little Understanding about God

There is another way we can give Satan entry into our lives. Jesus says, "When anyone hears the message about the kingdom and does not understand it, the evil one comes and snatches away what was sown in his heart" (Matthew 13:19). So understanding plays an important role in salvation. It also provides insulation from the enemy. Satan tries to reverse the process the Holy Spirit has started. The Spirit lights the fire of truth within us; the enemy tries to douse it. The reason Jesus emphasized the importance of understanding is that our belief in God is associated with what we know to be true about Him.

A minister I was talking with recently said, "We can never understand God." There is some truth to his statement, of course. Yet the entire Bible is God's way of trying to help us understand Him. God is not trying to hide Himself from us. And because we are finite, we will never know all there is to know about Him. But should this prevent us from hungering to know more? God says, "You will seek me and find me when you seek me with all your heart. I will be found by you" (Jeremiah 29:13–14). A seeker of truth recognizes God's Word as a way of understanding the Creator, while the minister's attitude is one reason the enemy can snatch away the good word that is sown.

It is no accident that following the Parable of the Sower (Matthew 13:1–9) is the Parable of the Weeds (verses 24–30). "The one who sowed the good seed," said Jesus, "is the Son of Man. The field is the world" (verse 37–38). Jesus recounted that "while everyone was sleeping, [the] enemy came and sowed weeds among the wheat" (verse 25). In the field both wheat and tares grew up together. The implication is that Satan does have influence in the world. The enemy, doing his work behind the cover of darkness, tries to destroy the good that the Father plants.

Reality Check

One of my sons and I were watching a movie on television one evening. He said, "Television isn't real, is it?" My first inclination was to say, "Of course not." Earlier, however, he had seen a program on wildlife, so I had to reconsider my response. I said, "Most of the programs on television aren't real."

This brief exchange left an impression on me. How is it that we decipher fact from fiction? Does art imitate life?

In the first dozen years of life, "the average child sees about 8,000 murders and 100,000 other acts of violence on television. . . . To argue that it has no impact goes counter to everything advertisers have researched about the medium."[8] One conclusive study of the influence of television violence was made by Dr. Leonard Eron, who wrote:

> There can no longer be any doubt that heavy exposure to televised violence is one of the causes of aggressive behavior, crime, and violence in society. Television violence affects youngsters of all ages, of both genders, at all socio-economic levels, and all levels of intelligence.[9]

Our world is full of counterfeits. This is one of Satan's most valuable weapons. He wants us to believe that what we see on the outside represents what is on the inside. According to Peter Marshall and David Manuel, "Satan is the master counterfeiter who is able to imitate every spiritual experience which a Christian can have, including the 'inner voice' of the Holy Spirit."[10] When we accept his counterfeits, our definition of values mirrors that of the secular culture. Satan tries to blind us, convincing us that appearance has preeminent significance.

Products designed to look and act like the original abound. I was replacing a ceiling fan in a friend's house one day when I bumped up against what I thought was a wood beam running the length of the room. It was plastic! For many years I had paneling on my office wall. It looked like wood but was only a picture of wood. Every day you and I use or see something that is meant to look real. Oak furniture usually consists of an oak veneer one sixteenth of an inch think glued to particle board. We have plastic plants, brick facades, fish that tastes like crab and margarine that tastes like butter. We buy look-alike computers and fake Rolex watches. Inevitably the counterfeit costs us less than the authentic.

Author Patricia McLaughlin points out the dangers of a status-driven culture. "Phony status symbols subvert a value system that's phony to begin with," she writes. "After all, don't we all believe we really ought to respect people for their virtues and achievements rather than their watches, pocketbooks and bank balances?" She concludes with a lesson for the church: "Counterfeits undermine the Rolex image of quality and dilute the effect of wearing the real thing."[11]

Our lust for what looks good, feels good or soothes our ego is insatiable. In our frenzy for more, we have lost the ability to tell the difference between the real and the imitation. And unreality in the material world can easily affect us in our moral lives, too. Jesus told the religious leaders, "You clean the outside of the cup and dish, but inside they are full of greed and self-indulgence" (Matthew 23:25). We have fallen into the image trap—failing to clean the inside while remaining shiny and polished on the outside.

Satan wants you and me to accept his counterfeit in our spiritual walk. He does not mind if we are religious so long as we do not influence anyone toward God. He wants us, like the Pharisees, to accept the *outward* manifestation of spirituality, which is far more effective in accomplishing his purpose of weakening the Church. As C. S. Lewis noted, "A moderated religion is as good as no religion at all."[12]

The apostle Paul exposed "false apostles, deceitful workmen" who disguised themselves as apostles of Christ (2 Corinthians 11:13). Undoubtedly some really did believe they were apostles. "Satan himself masquerades as an angel of light," reasoned Paul. "It is not surprising, then, if his servants masquerade as servants of righteousness" (verses 14–15).

When God's people begin to settle for a synthetic version of moral reality, there is no way the Church can gain strength. Satan wants to convince us that it is all right to be less than what God designed us to be, and his most skillful fraud often comes under the guise of religion. If he can get you and me to accept as holy those people who only *look* good, then our faith will begin to mirror theirs, and become weak and powerless.

Protect Yourself against the Enemy

> The knowledge that it is possible to be deceived keeps the mind open to truth and light from God.
>
> Jessie Penn-Lewis

How can we avoid the crafty and deceitful ways of our adversary? It takes more than simple knowledge of God's Word. It takes even more than being in His presence. Satan himself was in the presence of God—even worshiping Him!

He has seen holiness. He knows the difference between truth and error. He knows God's Word. He is skillful at imitating truth.

First, we need to be careful that we do not transfer complete responsibility for our spiritual growth to others. While this is necessary in spiritual infancy, eventually we need to walk on our own. Satan would love to see you turn your spiritual life over to someone else. You may assume that a pastor, teacher, evangelist or Bible scholar can know the truth for you. But some of Satan's greatest triumphs come from within the ranks of the Church. And those whose faith is built tenuously upon the spirituality of others cannot help falling.

I spoke with a man in his early forties who left his wife and family recently for another woman. He was struggling with guilt. He had grown up in a good church and knew he was living in rebellion to truth. Now he was starting to attend church once again, but he was still living with the other woman. He admitted to me that he did not value the favor of God more than anything else in his life—because, as he said, "I still have such strong feelings for her."

Did he think his emotions for her would disappear once he decided to come back to church? Many of us can be deceived about the power of our emotions. But we cannot play with them without eventually losing control of them at some point of weakness, like a runaway truck on a mountain road.

In most of the Northwest where I live, traveling over mountain passes is the most direct way between two points. These passes have signs warning trucks to reduce their downhill speed. When drivers see signs like this, do they think the highway patrol is inhibiting the potential of truck drivers? Of course not. They realize the signs are there for their good. They also see runaway truck ramps on the downward side of the mountain passes. These are for emergencies, in case the brakes fail. In general, if a truck driver is traveling faster than a safe speed, he puts himself (and other drivers) in danger. Our emotions work similarly. When we give in to them, they become difficult to control.

How do we protect ourselves against the enemy? At least four ways:

1. Control Your Thought Life

First, *gain and maintain control of your thought life.* The Bible says, "Prepare your minds for action . . ." (1 Peter 1:13). How do we do this? The next verse tells us: "Do not conform to the evil desires you had when you lived in ignorance" (verse 14). To be conformed means to agree in thought or idea, while God calls us to be different from what we were before we accepted Jesus.

2. Let God Search Your Heart

The second step is to protect yourself: *Be willing to let God search your heart.* In Scripture the heart is the seat of the will. It is the very core of a person. David said, "Search me, O God, and know my heart. . . . See if there is any offensive way in me" (Psalm 139:23–24). The process of maintaining a pure heart before God is essential to keeping the enemy at bay. Since the heart of man is "desperately wicked" (Jeremiah 17:9, KJV), we cannot completely trust ourselves. This is why we must be transparent before God and other trusted believers. The enemy wants us to think transparency is weakness. It is just the opposite. When we allow God to search us, it is liberating and produces spiritual growth and strength.

3. Make No Provision for the Enemy

A third step is to *make no provision for the enemy.* The Word says, "Lay aside the deeds of darkness and put on the armor of light. . . . Put on the Lord Jesus Christ, and make no provision for the flesh in regard to its lusts" (Romans 13:12, 14, NASB).

There are two parts to this verse. First we must be willing to lay aside the sinful activities that lead to self-deception and sin. When a person comes to Christ, he or she must be willing to put off the former way of living. We cannot give place continuously to the lusts of the flesh and live in subjection to God at the same time. The second part of the verse involves putting on "the armor of light." *Light* typically denotes truth or right guidance. The truth of God's Word is incorporated into our actions—a necessary element for protection.

4. Put On the Armor of God

The fourth step is to *put on the full armor of God.* This will help you "take your stand against the devil's schemes. For our struggle is not against flesh and blood, but against the rulers, against the authorities, against the powers of this dark world and against the spiritual forces of evil in the heavenly realms" (Ephesians 6:11–12).

Paul goes on in Ephesians 6 to describe the armor—seven different means of protection against the enemy.

BUCKLE ON TRUTH

The first piece of armor Paul mentions is *truth* (verse 14). Self-deception breeds when we are not fully committed to truth. And as we have seen, knowing truth and doing truth are not the same. Our determination to be lovers of truth, morally speaking, will keep us out of trouble and prevent Satan from having anything he can use against us as our accuser.

PUT ON RIGHTEOUSNESS

The second part of our armor is *righteousness* (verse 14). A holy life is a great frustration to Satan's plan. When we live according to God's design, it reinforces the cause of Christ and testifies to an unbelieving world. The saints in Revelation overcame Satan "by the blood of the Lamb and by the word of their testimony" (Revelation 12:11).

DO WHAT LEADS TO PEACE

A third part of our armor is the *preparation of the Gospel of peace* (verse 15). The truth often brings contention. Jesus experienced this with the Pharisees. There is a normal state of tension between those who practice immorality and those who stand for righteousness.

Constant contention, however, can provide a foothold for the enemy. We can be contentious through murmuring, gossip or argumentativeness. This does not help anyone, and the lack of peace diverts us from ministering to others and leaves us focused on our own problems. This does not mean we are to sacrifice the truth of God's Word to maintain a semblance of order. This is a form of denial. But Paul encourages us to "make every effort to do what leads to peace" (Romans 14:19).

HOLD UP THE SHIELD

The fourth element, *faith* (verse 16), enables us to stand fast under persecution and hardship. We can say with Job, "Though he slay me, yet will I trust in him" (Job 13:15, KJV). This unwavering trust and confidence in God frustrates Satan. We have faith that God has our lives in His hands. He is not ignoring us. Satan knows that the moral and spiritual stability of a believer hinders his work. He knows how difficult it is to distract this kind of believer.

PUT ON THE HELMET

Our fifth defense is the *helmet of salvation* (verse 17). It is significant that the helmet protects the head. Our emotions can go only in the direction that our thoughts allow them. Salvation, which begins with a conscious choice, protects our minds. It also means we are saved *from* something. Our salvation means we have accepted Christ by faith and have turned from our former way of life. This provides a cushion of insulation from the destruction our adversary desires to carry out in our lives. Our salvation grants us freedom from sin and death, which were part of our lives before we received Christ.

WIELD THE SWORD

The sixth safeguard against Satan is *the Word of God*, the sword of the Spirit (verse 17). Jesus responded to Satan's temptations in the wilderness by using God's Word. We, too, must know it if we are to use it to protect ourselves.

A sword is an offensive weapon. If it is left in its sheath, however, it is of no use. In Jesus' time, a soldier never went anywhere without first strapping on the leather belt that held his sword. He recognized that his life depended on it!

PRAY IN THE SPIRIT

Finally we are to *pray at all times in the Spirit* (verse 18). The Scripture adds, "On all occasions with all kinds of prayers and requests." These prayers fall into two classes— petition and praise. Prayer presupposes that God cares and that He will act for His people. Satan knows the power of praying believers and tries to thwart their prayers (recall Daniel 10). Prayer can serve as a protective hedge around those who acknowledge God, and the emphasis Jesus placed on prayer reminds us of its importance. Although the Lord was tired and busy, He always found time to commune with His heavenly Father. We must do the same.

We have discussed the subtle, destructive nature of self-deception. We have seen that it takes the form of excuses in our own lives or in the lives of friends or family members. But many Christians have a difficult time justifying, at least in their own minds, how God could seemingly bless the work or life of a person in self-deception and living a conspicuously sinful lifestyle.

In the next chapter we will answer an important question: Does God use people in self-deception? Then, in the remainder of Part 2, we will look at the "prescriptive" approach to deception—meaning how we or another believer can be set free from the stranglehold it can have on our Christian walk.

Chapter Highlights

- Satan is effective at blending truth and error. He presents partial truth, which often confuses us. We must apply the complete truth of God's Word to every aspect of our life, and adjust in areas in which we have made compromise.
- Christians are not immune to the cunning and deceptive tactics of Satan. The more we know about our enemy, the better prepared we will be.
- Satan tries to "subjectify" evil. He wants us to accept immorality as normal or permissible.
- The enemy tries to produce doubt about the absoluteness of God's Word. He weakens us through compromise and doubt.
- Satan manipulates the senses, encouraging us to give our time and energy to satisfy them.
- We become vulnerable to Satan when we leave areas of our life unprotected.
- Our adversary uses what looks good to trap us. As the chief counterfeiter, he wants us to accept a counterfeit spiritual walk.

Olber's Paradox

The naive and unscriptural belief that effective ministry is proof of righteous character is one of the most dangerous of all fallacies.

Don Basham

A young German named Wilhelm Olber was gazing into the sky one night in 1823. Countless stars glittered above the Bavarian landscape. But a perplexing thought crossed Olber's mind as he gazed upwards: *Why is the sky so dark?* Although it may seem a foolish question, Olber knew that each of the stars he could see was at least as large as our own sun. So, he reasoned, the night sky should be filled with light. The reason it is not, as Olber realized, is that each of the stars Olber saw was so much farther away than our own sun is.

The spiritual world demonstrates a similar paradox. What appears obvious in the spiritual realm, even more than in the physical realm, often is not.

A pastor in his mid-forties watches one Sunday morning as people from his small town flock into the front door of his church. He leans over to his associate minister and says, "You see all those people out there? That's God's way of saying He's pleased with us."

In another town that night, an evangelist opens the envelope that contains his honorarium check. His eyes grow wide with delight. It was a good night. He says to his wife, "You see, honey, the Lord is blessing our work."

On the other side of the world, a young missionary couple struggle through a meeting in the sweltering humidity of Delhi. They have not seen a single convert in eleven months. Their children are unhappy. Their apartment has no air conditioning. Last week they received word that one of their close friends was withdrawing his monthly support. The wife says to her husband, "Maybe coming to India wasn't God's will for us after all."

Many of us, like this pastor, evangelist and missionary couple, assume that prosperity is proof of God's blessing. Conversely, we believe that physical or financial hardship is evidence of God's disapproval. Both of these ideas are *sometimes* true. But often neither one is true.

A young pastor told David Wilkerson that Satan had held him for five years in the trap of adultery. "All the time that I was sinning, lying, cheating," explained the pastor, "my ministry prospered. God didn't seem angry. The offerings kept increasing; the blessings didn't stop. It seemed as if God were still with me in all I did."[1]

The pastor's story is no exception. Adultery, drunkenness, lying, manipulation and idolatry are no longer exclusive to the secular world. Laymen and pastors alike indulge in tax fraud, phone sex and illicit online relationships.

A Christian acquaintance of mine—we will call him John—decided he was tired of seeing his tax money not put to better use. Many of us, of course, would agree. But John took his frustrations one step farther. He stopped paying taxes altogether. While John's strategy worked for several years, it eventually caught up with him. The Internal Revenue Service confiscated everything he and his wife owned.

John has been playing a game of financial catch-up for years. He never interpreted his actions as "tax fraud." Instead he felt it was his right, possibly even his duty, to protest an unjust tax system.

The late Christian writer and columnist Jamie Buckingham wrote a powerful column titled "Philistines and the Media," in which he recounted:

> One TV preacher who drives a $100,000 automobile seemed genuinely baffled when he was criticized in the press as being "flamboyant." I asked him, "But why do you drive a $100,000 car?" He replied with a straight face, "A man in my kind of ministry needs good solid transportation."[2]

In an interview with *Modern Maturity*, former Atlanta mayor Andrew Young discussed his friend the Reverend Martin Luther King. Young, a minister himself, was asked why he never objected to accounts of Dr. King's extramarital affairs. "Because they are irrelevant," explained Young. "In public life, all that ought to be required is that your weaknesses don't interfere with your responsibilities."[3]

The obvious question for Young or any of us is whether an affair is relevant to those who suffer from the perpetrators' moral waywardness. And at least one of the purposes behind this chapter is to expose the fallacy that one's weaknesses and one's responsibilities are somehow disconnected. They are not. Not in private life and not in public life. This is a lesson many of our politicians have yet to learn. Private choices often do have public consequences. We cannot overlook private choices because we think they will be nullified by something grander. As Buckingham noted in his column,

> Values are not determined by who knows. They are absolute, even if no one else is watching. Unfortunately, stick-

ing with values because they are right—not because you might get caught—seems to be a fading character quality.[4]

From many of our pulpits we hear a gospel of cheap grace and divine tolerance. According to writer James Houston,

There is a moral leakage among us. . . . We are a nation of morally stillborn or, at best, morally retarded. The millions who say they are born again show little difference in regard to adultery, fornication, marital breakup, lying, tax evasion and other sins rampant in our society.[5]

Does God Use the Deceived?

Perhaps you, like me, have wondered why God does not intervene in these situations. Why does He allow people to go on misusing His name? Does He turn a blind eye to the behavior of some Christians because He needs them?

We will attempt to answer these important questions in the pages of this chapter. First let me emphasize, however, that just because you or I may not hold positions of spiritual authority does not mean we are not influenced by this false way of thinking. For us these questions must simply be asked differently. Do we think, for example, that our "good works" for the Lord—perhaps as deacons, visitation ministers or Sunday school teachers—counterbalance our unwillingness to obey Him? But even if we try to do good deeds only for those who need us, can we assume that the moral scale will tip in our favor if we do good to others while neglecting the most important relationship of all—the one with our Creator?

As we consider the question "Does God use the deceived?", there are two key words we need to define before going further. The first is *use*. In its most common form, *use* means "to put into action or service for a given purpose." Certain results may mirror God's work in our lives. In other words, what we say or do becomes the evidence of our love for God or others. Such actions are inseparable from our commitment to Christ. It is risky, however, to focus exclusively on the byproducts of our actions. They do not in themselves determine our spiritual fitness. It is easy to attach moral value to the results of our actions rather than valuing such qualities as obedience or solid moral character.

It is also easy to confuse the idea of use with that of potential. If my six-cylinder van is operating on just four cylinders, for example, I may reason, *It still works.* Just because my van is defective does not mean it cannot still get me where I need to go. This reasoning does not work, however, with moral issues. Although my van still works, its inefficiency is through no fault of its own, while a person in deception is morally responsible; he alone determines his spiritual condition through the choices he makes. This is what makes him different from the rest of creation. He is accountable to God for whatever conclusions he draws or actions he takes. When a gunman opens fire on a schoolyard, killing six children, no one says, "He's just not living up to his potential."

When we discuss the notion of use, we must consider whether God sanctions a particular action. By *sanction* I do not mean *punish.* Instead I am referring to whether God confirms or ratifies that action. This is the crux of the issue.

The second word we need to define is *self-deception.* We have been examining willful disobedience to known truth, as an individual intentionally accepts falsehood rather than obeys God's Word. It culminates in the redefinition of biblical truth to conform with that person's behavior or lifestyle choices. The principal characteristics of self-deception are habitual sin and excuse-making.

So let's reword the original question. Rather than ask, "Does God use the deceived?", let's ask, "Does God sanction the works of the deceived?" To understand the answer to this question, we must remember two aspects of God's character: *consistency* and *righteousness.* These two attributes weave a common thread through the following pages. The framework for our discussion, laid in previous chapters, helps us understand the inevitable question of how God operates through those living in sin or rebellion.

God Uses Imperfect Vessels

God's Word tells us that "all have sinned" (Romans 3:23). Few Christians debate this reality. The difficulty for some of us lies in understanding just how God uses us, flaws and all, to accomplish His purposes. And we get into trouble thinking that what we do for God sanctions our spiritual lives before Him. The fact is, we can be sure God does *not* endorse the efforts of those living in self-deception, if it means habitually or wantonly violating His own moral law. Nonetheless, God's Word, regardless of its source, often draws people to Him. As He says in Isaiah: "My word that goes out from my mouth . . . will not return to me empty, but will accomplish what I desire and achieve the purpose for which I sent it" (Isaiah 55:11).

David Wilkerson writes: "God closes heaven to those who break and flout His commandments. So what they preach (or say) has to come out of their own hearts and minds and can only be man-centered."[6] This is one of the frustrations that a person living in rebellion must grapple with. Like King David, such a person knows what it feels like to operate under the anointing or empowerment of the Lord. When that is gone, he must manufacture the anointing to continue ministering in the way he feels most comfortable. In so doing, he becomes a fraud. (This does not mean God does not use what is said by a teacher, preacher, singer or other Christian to draw people to Himself.)

Before a friend of mine received Christ, he was in what evangelist Charles Finney would call an "anxious state."

The Holy Spirit was convicting him of his sin. Tony spent a week secluded in the coastal mountains of California, lost his appetite and neither shaved nor bathed. Shortly after he returned home, he found a Russell's translation of the Bible used by the Jehovah's Witnesses. As he read, God began to reveal Himself. Because of Tony's hunger for truth, even a distortion of God's Word was enough to draw him to the Savior.

God is always faithful to meet a genuine seeker of moral or spiritual truth. The important question is, How do we respond to the prompting of the Holy Spirit?

Self-deception is generally more than a problem of a single moral transgression. It is the effort to disguise sin that becomes an act of rebellion. King David said, "If I regard wickedness in my heart, the Lord will not hear" (Psalm 66:18, NASB). The word *regard* means "to give attention or consideration." It refers to the state of one's heart. If God turns His face from a man or woman, how can that individual ever profess to speak for the Lord? And if that person is not speaking for the Lord, for whom is he or she speaking?

Self-deception prevents us from distinguishing God's voice from our own. He warns, "Do not listen to what the prophets are prophesying to you; they fill you with false hopes. They speak visions from their own minds, not from the mouth of the Lord" (Jeremiah 23:16). The prophets in Jeremiah's day were more than imperfect vessels. They were creating "words from the Lord" and controlling the people with them. The prophet Ezekiel wrote, "Their visions are false and their divinations a lie. They say, 'The LORD declares,' when the LORD has not sent them; *yet they expect their words to be fulfilled*" (Ezekiel 13:6, emphasis added). Why did they expect their words to be fulfilled? Because they thought they were speaking for God. They were unable to tell the difference between their own words and those spoken by Him.

Don't Misread the Signs

God used Samson to accomplish His purposes for the people of Israel and rescue them from the harassment of the Philistines. But Samson had his own agenda. When he killed, he did so out of revenge and anger. He married a Philistine woman against the wishes of his parents. And his lack of discipline led to self-indulgent living. When Samson was in the Philistine territory of Gaza one night to visit a prostitute, the Philistines heard he was in town and began making plans to kill him at dawn. But Samson arose in the middle of the night, tore the city gates from their foundation and carried them to the top of a nearby hill (see Judges 16:1–3).

Today many of us wonder how Samson could accomplish such a miraculous feat after arising from the bed of a harlot. How could God condone Samson's behavior by giving him victory over his enemies? Was Samson merely a vessel God used to accomplish His purposes?

Signs and wonders, as we have seen, are *not* the confirmation of God's blessing on an individual, church or ministry. This idea has its origins in our own culture. We esteem progress, products and accomplishments as if they possessed some intrinsic moral goodness, and we see quietness, stasis or delay as bad. In the secular marketplace, we value human beings according to might, money, acquisition or accomplishment. But God uses a different scale. His values have to do with motive, not results.

Are good results possible only when God is behind them? No. Can people receive salvation, healing or blessing through the life or ministry of a person in deception? Yes. Recall Jesus' warning:

> "Many will say to Me on that day, 'Lord, Lord, did we not prophesy in Your name, and in Your name cast out demons, and in Your name perform many miracles?' And then I will

declare to them, 'I never knew you; depart from Me, you who practice lawlessness.'"

Matthew 7:22–23, NASB

It is possible to operate completely in the flesh and still get results. You have seen this during altar calls. There are pastors and evangelists who can get people, weeping, to recite the sinner's prayer—but this does not mean the pastor or evangelist is right with God. We must not associate the results of one's efforts with his or her spirituality. The ability to control others can have an intoxicating effect, and eventually this becomes a way of life.

Like Samson, the people Jesus was talking about were getting results. Three times in one verse they said, "In Your name we did this or that." Yet the final judgment will come down on them: "Depart from Me!" Why? Because the self-deceived have a basic disregard for God's laws, His will and His ways.

We need to examine ourselves not on the basis of outward accomplishments but on the basis of inward motivation. If we do not, we deceive ourselves—if the outcome of our work or choices looks good—into thinking everything is O.K. Paul writes that rebellious people "reject the truth. . . . Their minds and consciences are corrupted. *They claim to know God*, but by their actions they deny him. They are detestable, disobedient and unfit for doing anything good" (Titus 1:14–16, emphasis added).

If we equate signs and wonders with God's blessing, the Egyptian diviners were godly men! They had the ability to replicate nearly every miraculous sign Moses and Aaron performed. Satan is a skillful counterfeiter. He, too, can perform signs and wonders. When we embrace the lie that miracles are proof of God's blessing, we set ourselves up for the spirit of Antichrist. During the end times Satan will perform "great and miraculous signs, even causing fire to come down from heaven to earth in full view of men" (Revelation 13:13). Jesus warns us, "False Christs and false prophets will appear and perform great signs and miracles to deceive even the elect—if that were possible" (Matthew 24:24). Even the most faithful and zealous among us must be on guard.

Can some people walking in deception continue to show positive results in their personal lives, ministries or churches? Is it possible to have bad deeds and good results? Paul uses the word *deed* interchangeably with *exploit* or *feat*. If we measure *good result* as a completed project or the number of people in our church, the answer is yes. Paul's words *detestable* and *disobedient* show that these people were unwilling to heed the word of the Lord. Their deeds were proof of their unwillingness to follow His ways.

This leads us back to the question of this chapter: Why does God allow people like Samson to misrepresent Him? Why doesn't He stop them? When Christians using God's name bring disrepute and judgment on the Church, it leaves many of us feeling disappointed, helpless, even hopeless. Yet God does not act or respond according to our time frame. He is patient with us and does not interfere with the freedom He has given us, even when He is hurt by that freedom. We must acknowledge, without compromising His sovereignty, that all Scripture is God's way of revealing Himself to us. He wants to be known by us, even if it is through the ministry of someone in rebellion against Him.

Maybe you are wondering, *If God were to approve the works of the rebellious, wouldn't He be agreeing to the very lawlessness He abhors?* This is what you and I are suggesting when we attribute our own works to God. So why doesn't God stop us? The answer has nothing to do with God's grace, longsuffering or willingness to ignore sin. It rests, rather, in the issue of man's freedom. If I give my son the keys to my car, it does not mean I will condone the way he uses it. You might ask, "Aren't you an irresponsible father, then, for giving him the keys?" I don't think so—even though I freely acknowledge the risks associated with giving my son freedom.

For His own sovereign reasons, God rarely intervenes in our decisions, even when we misrepresent Him. He has given us freedom to sin or to obey, and will rarely interfere with the decisions you and I make. This is the nature of freedom—the ability to originate and carry out actions without interference.

Process and Progress

British journalist Malcolm Muggeridge once said, "The great fallacy of our time is the one that says we may pursue collective virtue apart from personal behavior." The person in deception believes God overlooks his or her behavior for some grander plan. But when we assume God's primary interest is in our accomplishments, we minimize the *process.* Christ calls you and me to *be* His disciples. As Jesus said, "Whoever serves me must follow me; and where I am, my servant also will be" (John 12:26). The act of being is more difficult than the process of doing—even though we are doers, and doing is the way we prefer to assess our value as individuals. We wind up placing more value on our good work *for* Him than our obedience *to* Him.

Oswald Chambers addressed the preeminence of being over doing:

> Beware of anything that competes with loyalty to Jesus Christ. The greatest competitor of devotion to Jesus is service to Him. The one aim of the call of God is the satisfaction of God, not a call to do something for Him.[7]

Then there is the issue of *progress.* When we elevate progress above all else, we lose sight of God's values. This is the preamble to situation ethics. It is false moral logic to say that an act is virtuous because the results are favorable. God is interested not in the success or failure of a ministry as much as He is in accomplishing His purposes in individuals.

The stories of Samson and King Saul are examples of how God uses people in spite of their disobedience. Our degree of obedience is always a measure of our consecration to God. When we disobey Him, we demonstrate our disregard for His will. Whenever we elevate ministry or self above obedience to God, we proclaim progress as a pre-eminent virtue. When the ends justify the means, we honor the god of situation ethics. In such a state we can excuse anything on the basis of external success.

God has designed you and me to derive satisfaction from serving Him through what we do. This is both natural and normal. Our work or ministry is a form of service to Him. Nevertheless, this can lead to a false sense of God's acceptance, which is why it is dangerous to equate our accomplishments with God's acceptance. Such thinking winds its way into our perception of salvation.

This is not to say that doing things for the Lord is of little value. When we care for the homeless, take in orphans or give to missions, we are serving Him. But our actions must emanate from a heart to please the Lord and do His will. What we do for God must proceed from relationship with Him, rather than the other way around.

The apostle Paul wrote that every person's work

> will be shown for what it is, because the Day will bring it to light. It will be revealed with fire, and the fire will test the quality of each man's work. If what he has built survives, he will receive his reward. If it is burned up, he will suffer loss; he himself will be saved, but only as one escaping through the flames.
>
> 1 Corinthians 3:13–15

Paul also wrote, "Whatever you do, work at it with all your heart, as working for the Lord, not for men, since you know that you will receive an inheritance from the Lord as a reward. It is the Lord Christ you are serving" (Colossians 3:23–24).

Our spiritual bank account fills up when we do our work with the right intention of heart. All other work, whether it produces good results or not, has no spiritual virtue.

Fruit and Fables

The following comments accompany Jesus' admonition to bear fruit:

> "I am the true vine, and my Father is the gardener. He cuts off every branch in me that bears no fruit, while every branch that does bear fruit he prunes so that it will be even more fruitful. You are already clean because of the word I have spoken to you. Remain in me, and I will remain in you. No branch can bear fruit by itself; it must remain in the vine. Neither can you bear fruit unless you remain in me.
> "I am the vine; you are the branches. If a man remains in me and I in him, he will bear much fruit; apart from me you can do nothing."
>
> John 15:1–5

What did Jesus mean when He spoke of fruit? Not simply works, progress or accomplishment, even though, for many, the words *fruit* and *results* are the same. We refer to an accomplishment as "the fruit of one's labor."

If Jesus referred only to accomplishments, then signs and wonders would certainly fit this definition. But fruit is more than works. It is more than results. John the Baptist told the Pharisees to "produce fruit in keeping with repentance" (Matthew 3:8). John was saying, "If you really love God, then act like it!" Fruit consists of character traits that result in our becoming more like Christ—qualities like love, joy, peace, patience, kindness, goodness, faithfulness, gentleness and self-control (see Galatians 5:22–23). Jesus was saying that unless these qualities are part of your life, your works are in vain. Author Juan Carlos Ortiz writes, "Gifts do not indicate spirituality. . . . People fool themselves by seeking the Spirit's gifts instead of His fruit."[8]

173

How, then, can God use people when they have aligned themselves against His purposes? Since God must be true to His own Word, *He does not endorse the lifestyle or ministry of those who are in rebellion to Him.* This leaves us with yet another question. Suppose a woman is an effective evangelist or teacher. If she sins, does God withdraw her ability to teach or reach others for Christ?

Paul answers this question: "God's gifts and his call are irrevocable" (Romans 11:29). This simple truth explains much. God does not withdraw a gift from someone who sins or even someone who is in deception. Don Basham wrote, reasoning from Romans 11:29: "Since the gifts and anointing of God are not given because a man behaves properly, neither are they taken away because a man behaves improperly."[9] Again, we mistakenly link the use of a gift with the anointing of God—and this is precisely where we get into trouble. We look at ourselves or others and base our spiritual judgments on the wrong criteria.

It is important to look at the fruit connected to a gift or ministry and identify the source of it. The proper use of spiritual gifts is always accompanied by humility and it always demonstrates love and points toward God.

When the people of Lystra began to worship Paul and Barnabas after God healed a lame man, the apostles tore their clothes and said, "We too are only men, human like you. We are bringing you good news, telling you to turn from these worthless things to the living God" (Acts 14:15). Earlier in the growth of the Church, when Peter and John were instruments of healing to a lame man, Peter said to the crowds, "Why do you marvel at this . . . as if by our own power or piety we had made him walk?" (Acts 3:12, NASB).

When we misuse God's gifts, we are elevating self and breaking the first commandment, which forbids idolatry of any kind. Those in deception may act as if they are giving God the glory. But, like the Pharisees, they are seeking the attention of others. Rather than give glory to God, their actions draw men and women to themselves. In every instance of the legitimate use of God's gifting, on the other hand, the glory goes to God. The person who walks in humility inevitably turns people toward the Source of the blessing.

We have seen in this chapter how risky it is to focus on the results of our work, ministry or accomplishments. Once a person is caught in the web of self-deception, it is difficult to get free. The problem is that a person's perception of moral or spiritual godliness becomes twisted through wrong choices. So in the next chapter we will focus on how to reverse the process of self-deception.

Chapter Highlights

- God does not remove a spiritual gift, regardless of our sin or disobedience. His gifts are irrevocable.
- Since all people are sinners, God must accomplish His purposes through imperfect vessels. This does not mean, however, that God approves of the behavior or lifestyle of those walking in disobedience.
- Personal, business or ministry success does not indicate that a person is on good terms with God. Nor does failure in any of these suggest that a person is in disobedience to God.
- We cannot judge our own spiritual health or that of others exclusively by the positive external results of our life. The only true gauge for spiritual health is Galatians 5:22–23.
- God rarely overrides man's free will to accomplish His purposes, either personally or corporately.
- God values obedience above the results of our actions or activities.

Pushing the Envelope

Catch for us the foxes, the little foxes that ruin the vineyards.

Song of Songs 2:15

We've surrendered our lives to the momentum of mediocrity.

Marlon Brando

For the past seven years Jane has managed a major department with the county. Her friends and colleagues know she is a born-again Christian. Perhaps because she is outgoing and affable, she was recruited by another Christian to sell a line of cleaning products. In debt and looking for a way to bolster her income, Jane caught the vision immediately. She attended every seminar possible and gleaned what she could from her new mentors. It did not take long before Jane was talking to everyone she knew about the line of products. Friends, family and colleagues soon found themselves listening to her sales pitch. She even began using her office and position as an avenue for sales. Eventually Jane lost her job.

Unlike Jane, who worked in a secular job, Sandra has spent 25 years serving different Christian ministries. She is sharp, witty and good with people. Her position of influence has landed her on several ministry boards. She understands what it takes to make a ministry work: people. Not just any people, but donors. And Sandra knows lots of them. Through the years she has gleaned donor names from the ministry she works for and given them to other ministries.

Perhaps you are thinking that what Jane and Sandra have done is a simple conflict of interest. It is that. But it is much more.

Or maybe you think it is no big deal. Let me engage in a bit of rationalization in both cases. If I am Jane, I might place the blame for my dismissal on "ungodly county officials." In Jane's mind, she became a martyr for the cause of Christ. And Sandra might be thinking, *I'm helping other worthy ministries by networking them to godly needs.* It sounds good, doesn't it?

It is easy to look at big ethical or moral issues and say to ourselves, *I'd never do that.* In most instances you probably wouldn't. Most of us do not sleep with our neighbor's wife or steal from his garage. This chapter is not about this kind of activity. It is about the "little stuff," the little foxes that spoil the vineyard. In the Arab world there is a saying: "If you let the camel put its nose into your tent, you will soon be sleeping with it." Morally speaking this chapter is about keeping the camel's nose out of your tent.

Identifying Gray Areas

I have noticed that in north Idaho, church attendance drops dramatically each fall. Many of the women come to church alone or only with their daughters, while many of the men engage in a back-to-nature ritual called hunting. For days or weeks, men and their sons brave the rugged elements of the wilderness. I have noticed something else. The *No Hunting* and *No Trespassing* signs are often either ignored or pockmarked by buckshot.

This past fall I closed and locked the gate to my property. Within a few days local hunters driving all-terrain vehicles were steering around the locked gate and through a broken piece of barbed wire. Since I am interested in why people do what they do, I asked myself, *Is it possible my neighbors don't read?* But even if they don't, how hard can it be to interpret the meaning of a locked gate? I am not sure why people deliberately ignore signs or rules. I think it has to do with a mentality that reasons something like this: "The *No Trespassing* and *No Hunting* signs are there for other people. Since we've hunted here for twenty years, we have a right to be here." Local hunters may even appreciate the fact that I locked the gate to keep "other" intruders out of their hunting ground.

Are there activities or thoughts you have taken for granted? Maybe you feel you have a right to trespass certain of God's laws. Maybe you believe you are entitled to think, feel or behave in a certain way that is not necessarily desirable or even acceptable for other people. Perhaps you see certain issues as trivial compared to "serious" offenses. Instead of looking at this chapter as nitpicking, legalistic, or my attempt to lay a guilt trip on you, please use it as a way to honestly examine any gray areas in your life.

I will explain later why these areas are more serious than you might think. But first it is important to recognize that nearly all of us have these blind spots. If we ask God or those close to us to honestly help identify these, God will be faithful to help us change our thinking.

When Do We Slip?

Gray areas have a tendency to appear whenever we find ourselves backed into a corner. Not long ago I received a phone call from a saleswoman when I was busy on another project and did not want to be interrupted. I asked my wife,

Sue, to take a message because I did not want to talk to the woman. When she called back fifteen minutes later, however, I went ahead and spoke with her. At the end of the conversation I said, "Thanks for calling. It was good to talk with you." As I hung up the phone, I heard a fellow employee within earshot snickering. She knew I had not wanted to talk with the saleswoman, and she found my less-than-honest response humorous. Then I recognized that in my simple attempt to be polite, I was lying.

Gray areas also crop up when we want something badly enough. We have a general rule in our family, for example, that we will not rent or view R-rated movies. Why? It is easier for me to compromise my values when there is a movie I really want to see. To the extent that I can satisfy my conscience through compromise, my values begin to break down. Compromise usually simmers in the caldron of desire.

We also tend to compromise when we feel we have been treated unjustly. This often occurs within a marriage or in the workplace. If my boss is a tyrant, or if I have had to work too much overtime, I may take longer lunch breaks, justify my use of the office phone for personal calls, or "borrow" office supplies or equipment.

We tend to sacrifice the truth when it serves us or someone with whom we are connected. The assurance that "the check is in the mail" has become a joke because it is misused by people who have *not* put a check into the mail. I was surprised to hear a secretary I know tell a caller that her boss had just left, when we both knew very well he was in the office next door. In her mind she was protecting him from intrusion. But since that episode I have never completely trusted this secretary when she tells me something.

Exaggeration, manipulation or outright lying in sales positions is common. Some people think it is impossible to be competitive without distorting the truth to some degree. But we can be confident that God will always honor truth and honesty. The business of truth, sad to say, is not as valued as it once was. Our own government encourages a form of deception through policies like "Don't ask, don't tell." The author of an article titled "In Defense of the Little White Lie" says,

> Sometimes bending the truth can be smart, even noble. Yes, lies can be manipulative or compulsive, but some spare feelings, relieve worries, or get us past our overwrought situations without pointless confrontation.[1]

Salesmen struggling to make ends meet may find it easier to leave out crucial details to prospective buyers or, as is often the case with salespeople, to try to convince them to buy a more expensive car, a bigger house, a nicer dress. When we serve to benefit in some way from a lie or partial truth, we cannot always trust ourselves to make a sound moral judgment free from partiality. This does not mean the truth might not cost us a business deal, important account or sale. It simply means that doing what is right is our first and only option.

My friend Lee Grady, executive editor of *Charisma* magazine, told me they have a policy of not mixing editorial with advertising. That is a wise moral decision. Can you imagine someone saying, "I'll buy a page of advertising if you'll run a story on my ministry." The temptation would be to say, "What's the harm?" In the long run, however, making editorial decisions based on advertising commitments undermines the integrity of a publication. Other Christian magazines will not run a book review unless the publisher or author buys ad space. To me this is a conflict of interest motivated by economic concerns.

Because we may be ignorant of gray areas in our lives, we need to be open to the counsel of others. We also need to allow the Holy Spirit to bring these areas to our mind, then convict us. Let me give an example. For years, whenever I found an uncanceled postage stamp on a package or envelope, I peeled it off and reused it. Then I was startled by a notice at the local post office that said something like this: *Reusing uncanceled stamps is a violation of federal law.* I could have rationalized, *There have been times when my postage meter misfired, so I'm just paying myself back.* Instead I discontinued the practice. In this case, the realization that my previous actions were wrong produced an immediate change in my behavior.

Our Choices Are Bigger Than We Are

A note from a close friend illustrates the truth that our choices are bigger than we are. "I was getting a perm last Friday," she wrote, "from a nice woman who told me that her plans to go to St. Thomas had been thwarted when her travel companion had to work. Then she revealed that her friend was an Episcopal priest. My tongue loosened by this revelation, I asked, 'Doesn't the church have a problem with his going to St. Thomas with a female friend?' I guess I hoped she'd say with a laugh, 'Oh, we had separate rooms.' Instead she bristled a little. 'What he does on his own time is his own business,' she said coolly."

What any follower of Christ does on "our own time," either directly or indirectly, represents the One we serve. While it might be convenient to think we can compartmentalize our lives, this is hypocritical since our behavior affects others. And since action follows belief, what we do on our own time, our employer's time or anyone else's time *is* God's business.

A recent example illustrates the extent to which our choices are bigger than we are. Gary, a deacon at his church, has spent the past twelve years working as a county employee. His female supervisor, though not a Christian, has a reputation of being competent, fair and honest. But a few weeks ago, just before he left for a few days of vacation,

Gary filed a $1 million claim against the county for reverse sexual discrimination—a claim some people believed was motivated by personal greed.

The point at issue in this chapter is not whether Gary has a scriptural right to sue the county. It is not even whether he has a justifiable claim against his supervisor. Rather, let's consider the question of how his actions reflect his faith. An unbeliever in another county office remarked, "Gary's actions don't seem like a very Christian thing to do."

Regardless of the circumstances of Gary's case, his choices are bigger than he is. They will affect taxpayers and influence very public attitudes toward Christians in general, toward Gary's church, toward his supervisor, even toward the county. And his actions will color the way individuals throughout the county view the local leadership.

Satan does his best to create tension or conflict in our social relationships. To the extent that he is successful at keeping families, churches, businesses, teams or governments in turmoil, Satan diverts us from becoming the influencers in our world that God desires. Like Gary, we can be unwitting instruments of Satan by failing to recognize the gray areas in our lives.

Deceptive Communication

In marriage, family and relationships, gray areas generally take the form of deflection, withholding information and half-truths. In families, children and spouses "protect" each other from the truth, because the truth often brings up more questions, which can get them into deeper trouble. These varieties of miscommunication are all forms of deception.

When our children do not want to tell us what they are up to, they use deflection. A conversation might sound something like this:

Parent: Where have you been?
Child: Nowhere.
Parent: What do you mean, nowhere?
Child: I was out.
Parent: Who were you out with?
Child: Friends.

You can see this conversation is going nowhere fast. The child will not answer the questions directly. He diverts.

The same thing happens in marriages, and this is usually learned behavior. One spouse overreacts; the other spouse begins to withhold communication. Some spouses do not want to take the time to communicate at all. Since our tendency is to avoid conflict, lack of communication, often in the form of partial truth, becomes a mechanism to keep the peace.

In her book *Lying: Moral Choice in Public and Private Life,* Sissela Bok devotes entire chapters to deceptive communication. These include lying in a crisis, lying to liars, lying to enemies, lying to protect peers and clients, lying for the public good, paternalistic lies and lies to the sick and dying. In each of Bok's categories, we can see how simple it is to justify withholding important information from a boss, friend, colleague or child. Isn't it easier, for example, to mislead our boss into thinking we have carried out her instructions rather than face her with the truth? Perhaps, we may reason, we can buy ourselves more time to get the job done. Surely no one will be harmed by our deceptive communication. But at the very least we harm ourselves, since little lies often lead to greater deception.

Guardians of the Truth

My oldest son went to a newspaper machine recently with the two quarters I gave him to buy a paper. Before inserting the coins, he lifted the handle and discovered that it was not latched. He could have said, *Thank You, Lord, for providing this free paper for my dad today and letting me keep these quarters.*

The test of moral character is what you do in a given situation when you know you can benefit by something that is not quite right and still not be discovered. Moral character is forged in the alleys and back roads of anonymity. Milton wrote, "I cannot praise a fugitive and cloistered virtue, unexercised and unbreathed." One way to be sure we pass our tests is to keep the foxes out of the vineyards. This means we keep the moral gates to our vineyards locked, because it is always easier to keep the foxes out than to chase them out after they have already gotten in.

If *Money* magazine is right, Americans are more likely than ever to cheat a waiter by failing to correct a wrongly added bill, underpay their taxes and keep a cash-loaded wallet found on the street.[2] According to James Patterson in *The Day America Told the Truth*, Americans cheat more, lie more, are unfaithful and self-centered. The way we can make a difference in the midst of these depressing realities is to be different. If we lower ourselves to the morality of a self-serving society, our faith will mean nothing to those who need Jesus Christ.

As Francis Schaeffer put it, "We are surrounded by a society with no fixed standards and 'no fault' everything. Each thing is psychologically pushed away or explained away so there is no right or wrong."[3] He asks, "Why do we have so little impact on the world today?" The answer, in part, is that many of us have failed to assume our responsibility as guardians of the truth in our own lives. We have not been faithful in the smaller things.

I used to work with a man who signed his letters *Dr. Jim.* Jim was no Ph.D. In fact, I am not sure he ever completed high school. But rather than feel ashamed for acting like a phony, he took pride in it. To someone who has spent eight years in higher education, Dr. Jim's title is an affront to reality and truthfulness.

In his book about ethics, Robertson McQuilkin makes this statement about integrity:

> Integrity may be the most precious possession I have, its violation my greatest loss. Can I be trusted? If not, all other virtues become uncertain. Lack of integrity is a fault-line in the character that jeopardizes all other values and undermines all relationships.[4]

The question of integrity is an important one for the Body of Christ. If we cannot be trusted, we cannot honestly expect people to risk becoming vulnerable to the Church or to her doctrines. Integrity can be summed up by asking ourselves this question: "Have I done what I said I would do?" It really is that simple. Either our word is good or it is not. As McQuilkin pointed out, it is a matter of being trustworthy.

In past generations, transactions were handled with a handshake, but today most people see conducting meaningful business this way as foolhardy. In my own public relations business I avoid lengthy agreements or contracts and use a letter of agreement instead. Occasionally a client wants a "to-the-letter" contract, but this is usually because they have been burned by someone in the past.

Some of the synonyms for integrity are *soundness, completeness, honesty* and *incorruptibility.* These describe the moral qualities of individuals, churches, businesses and nations. Our integrity—which is part of our character—is developed through the choices we make. And since every Christian is called to be a lover of the truth, we must guard it by being doers of the truth. Any form of moral compromise violates truth and undermines integrity.

When Absolutes Are Hard to Find

Some situations are not as cut and dried as we would like. Under such conditions, what are we to do? How do we decide on issues that are not clear cut? What criteria should we use?

Perhaps this is a good starting place: *When you are faced with a moral decision, do you see how far you can go without overtly sinning?* Seeing how far you can go is a risk, since the lines between right and wrong get blurry when we are walking on the edge. And standing on the edge of a moral cliff, as we have already seen, is far riskier than keeping a safe distance.

As an alternative to this philosophy, I pose what I have labeled the Moral Acceptability Test. These are seven questions to ask when you are struggling with a decision that may have moral consequences:

1. Is it legal?
2. Will it hurt me or others?
3. If I don't act, will others be hurt?
4. Could it be a stumblingblock to other Christians?
5. Could it hurt the cause of Christ?
6. Have I consulted with other godly Christians about it?
7. Do I feel compelled to explain my decision to others?

All of these questions contain pitfalls. A certain action may be legal, for example, but cause the name of Christ to come into disrepute. Likewise, just because a certain action may hurt another person does not necessarily mean we should not do it. Asking other Christians about a course of action may also be risky, which is why we need to choose our moral advisors wisely. But these are general rules, and most of the time general rules work well when we are faced with a moral dilemma.

Let's apply these questions to Gary's case mentioned earlier.

Is It Legal?

Is it legal to sue the county? The answer is obviously yes. As a follow-up: Is it right for a Christian to sue an unbeliever? On this point there is some debate. Is the scriptural injunction against taking your brother to court (see 1 Corinthians 6:1–8) just between believers, or does it apply to both believers and unbelievers? Could it be argued that Gary *was* taking other believers to court, since many believers would have to pay the suit through their tax money? It gets complicated. Generally speaking, the more complicated a moral dilemma is, the more motivated we ought to be to avoid the confusion.

Will It Hurt Others?

Will Gary's suit hurt others? The answer to this second question is clear: Gary's action against the county will hurt taxpayers.

We might then ask, for question #3: If Gary does not act, will others be hurt? If the suit is legitimate, does the supervisor's behavior hurt others? We could apply the same question to saving the life of a drowning child by jumping over a fence that says *No Trespassing.* If our inaction will cause others to suffer, we should act. There is no indication that Gary's inaction will hurt others unless we argue that he is protecting future employees from being mistreated—although this might be a bit of a stretch.

Could It Be a Stumblingblock?

To the fourth question: Will his actions be a stumblingblock to others? The answer is clear. Gary's actions have already influenced the way unbelievers see him as an individual and how they view the influence of Christianity in his life.

Could It Hurt the Cause of Christ?

As to the fifth question, Gary's choices have definitely had a negative effect on the cause of Christ, because some who know he is a Christian say they think less of Christianity as a result. This is summed up in a commonly heard statement: "If this is how Christians act, I want nothing to do with Christianity."

Have I Consulted with Others?

The sixth question may be one of the most important. Gary failed to consult brothers or sisters in Christ about the decision before he took action. If you are not sure about which course of action to take, ask a godly friend or two, or talk with your pastor. Be sure these friends understand all the facts, so their counsel is not based on incomplete information. Since most of us do not feel neutral about our decisions, we need to guard against bias.

Do I Have to Explain My Decision?

The final question deals with our inclination to explain our decisions. Gary became a lobbyist for his own cause. When we find ourselves on precarious moral ground, we search instinctively for allies or sympathizers who can unwittingly bolster our position. When you find yourself trying hard to explain your point of view, this is strong evidence that you are making a wrong decision.

In this chapter we have looked at what we can do to guard against the subtleties of self-deception in ourselves. In the final section of this book, we will take a serious look at the issue of self-deception in others. What can we do when someone has so compromised the absoluteness of

God's Word that he or she cannot see the situation as others do? While confrontation is indeed necessary at times, the ultimate responsibility for change lies within the individual in cooperation with the Holy Spirit.

Chapter Highlights

- Identifying moral blind spots can prevent us from getting into more serious sin.
- Gray areas are moral areas or decisions that may not be based upon scriptural absolutes.
- Deflection, withholding information and half-truths are all forms of deception.
- Integrity is doing what you say you will do or what you have already agreed to do.
- When making a moral decision, check with other godly people and run it through the seven questions in the Moral Acceptability Test.

PART 3

From Darkness into Light

Removing the Scales

Encourage one another daily, as long as it is called Today, so that none of you may be hardened by sin's deceitfulness.

Hebrews 3:13

God's truth and the work of Christ's church both insist that truth demands loving confrontation, but confrontation.

Francis Schaeffer

Janice, a missionary in her early forties, grew up with an alcoholic father. "I know he's an alcoholic," Janice told me. "He just won't admit it." He came home from work at night and guzzled beer. A can was never far from reach. Yet he could not bring himself to admit what everyone in his family already knew.

We have a similar problem when we do not want to admit that something is off track in our lives. We either ignore it, repress it or excuse it. We may even dismiss immoral behavior by relabeling it, removing personal responsibility and any motivation to change.

There are three manifestations of the moral hardening that Hebrews 3:13 speaks about:

1. The refusal to acknowledge a problem or sin
2. An unwillingness to deal with a problem or sin that one does recognize
3. A lethargic, hesitant or unwilling attitude toward getting help

We have looked so far at how deception can create problems in our lives as individual believers in Jesus Christ. In this chapter we will pursue some of the ways we can help someone else break free from self-deception. Another title for this chapter could be "A Case for Confrontation." Whether we like it or not, the Bible is a book about confrontation. The message of the cross, at the core of Christianity, is about confronting sin and evil.

Let's start by considering an ability without which we would all be vulnerable to deception.

Discernment: The Key to Understanding

Discernment is the capacity to differentiate between separate or competing possibilities. To discern effectively requires judgment, insight and perception. Suppose you went to a department store to purchase a new suit or dress. How would you know which is the best? Most of us go through an immediate diagnostic process. We look at the material, color, label, cost and fit. Our final decision might include other variables, including previous purchases from the same manufacturer and comments by a friend or salesperson.

Can we learn to become as discerning in our Christian faith as we are in our shopping? There are at least two steps to increasing discernment in our lives.

Ask

The first step to becoming a discerning Christian is *to ask.* King Solomon prayed, "Give your servant a discerning heart to govern your people and to distinguish between right and wrong" (1 Kings 3:9). God's response to Solomon was positive: "Since you have asked for this and not for long life or wealth for yourself . . . but for discernment in administering justice, I will do what you have asked" (verse 11–12).

God wants to give you and me a discerning heart as He did Solomon. But we must put discernment above riches, honor or glory. If we do, God will respond favorably.

While Solomon's life is an example of how to gain discernment, it is also a warning of how easily we can lose it. Disobedience to God's Word cost this great king his ability to discern:

> King Solomon . . . loved many foreign women . . . from nations about which the LORD had told the Israelites, "You must not intermarry with them, because they will surely turn your hearts after their gods." Nevertheless, Solomon held fast to them in love. . . . As Solomon grew old, his wives turned his heart after other gods, and his heart was not fully devoted to the LORD his God.
>
> 1 Kings 11:1–2, 4

Solomon did not lose his ability to discern overnight. The process took place over many years. Those in self-deception, as with Solomon, find their ability to discern dwindling slowly. The compromise of God's Word gradually prevents them from seeing their lives or choices from God's perspective.

Judge Rightly

The second part of becoming a discerning Christian is *learning to judge rightly*. Jesus said, "Stop judging by mere appearances, and make a right judgment" (John 7:24). What did Jesus mean by *right judgment?*

Many of us are hung up about this. It is a touchy subject. We say, "Only God can judge," or, "It's not our business." Unfortunately, our unwillingness to judge within the Body of Christ is producing an anemic Church. The confusion surrounding judging comes from cultural taboos and the misreading of Scripture. In some instances this misunderstanding is perpetuated by those who do not wish to be the source of scrutiny themselves.

The main misinterpretation comes from Jesus' own words in the Sermon on the Mount: "Judge not, that ye be not judged" (Matthew 7:1, KJV). There appears to be an inconsistency between this verse and Jesus' admonition for us to "make a right judgment." But if we read what follows the "Judge not" verses, a more complete picture unfolds. Jesus makes it clear *when* to judge, not *whether* to judge. We judge righteously when we do so without hypocrisy or malice, and with the motive to restore.

The apostle Paul was straightforward in passing judgment on the man living in an incestuous relationship within the Corinthian church. If Paul himself had been living in sexual immorality, his judgment would have been hypocritical. Even so, some believers argue, "We are all sinners," implying that *any* judgment of another person is wrong. Others add, echoing the hairdresser's defense of the priest in the previous chapter, "What I do with my life is no one's business. It's between me and God."

But this is not the way God intends His Church to function. Moral vitality is the result of maintaining a set of standards that everyone follows. These standards, as we have seen, are based on God's moral expectations laid out in Scripture.

Why Are We to Judge?

A tragic mistake many well-meaning Christians make is assuming they can get people to change. It makes no difference what your motive is; people must come to their own decisions. The purpose of confrontation, then, is not to force people to change, or even to get them to think as we do, but to bring them to a place where they recognize their need to conform to God's standards, and then be willing to do so.

There are at least four reasons we must be willing to confront sin in another person.

1. Love for One Another

First, we must be willing to confront sin or error because of our love for the other person. Some argue, "But you're trying to take the place of the Holy Spirit in that person's life." Yet some believers have not learned to listen to the Holy Spirit. Others simply ignore Him. Whether we like it or not, we are our brother's keeper. And when we excuse his sinful behavior, we ignore an important element of love. Real love is not passive acceptance of sin. Love is active, nurturing, encouraging and merciful. At times it also involves confrontation.

If we love God and His Word, then sinful behavior, regardless of who does it, must be dealt with. And when we face sin, it always involves making a moral judgment.

2. Love for God

Another reason we must confront sin is our love for God and His reputation. David Wilkerson asks, "Why do we not have as much concern about the honor of Christ as we do for the reputations of our preachers?"[1] Many Christians purport that we are not God's advocates and that He can take care of Himself. But this was not the attitude Moses had when he pleaded with God not to destroy the children of Israel: "Why should the Egyptians say, 'It was with evil intent that [God] brought them out, to kill them in the mountains and to wipe them off the face of the earth'?" (Exodus 32:12). After this remarkable intervention, an appeal to God on behalf of His own reputation, God responded positively.

Every aspect of a believer's life reflects on God in one way or another. It is important to represent Him in a manner worthy of our calling as His children. To do otherwise is to open the floodgates of criticism on the Church.

3. To Help Deter Sin

The apostle Paul wrote, "When Peter came to Antioch, I opposed him to his face, because he was clearly in the wrong" (Galatians 2:11). Paul went on to say that he confronted Peter "in front of them all" (verse 14). While Paul may not have been worried about some blatant immorality, Peter was clearly guilty of acting like a hypocrite. Paul was concerned because Peter's behavior influenced other Jews to join him in his hypocrisy. Even Barnabas, one of Paul's previous traveling companions, was led astray by Peter.

Another important reason to judge, therefore, is the deterrent effect it has on others. Paul writes, "Those who continue in sin, rebuke in the presence of all, so that the rest also may be fearful of sinning" (1 Timothy 5:20, NASB). Several words stand out in this verse. First, the phrase *continue in sin*. The entire discussion of self-deception hinges on repetition. In most instances it is unwise to expose sin publicly. Sin must be habitual to fit this exposure criterion. This does not mean we ignore one-time sin. It simply means we treat habitual sin more seriously, because the long-term effects are more serious.

The second important word in this verse is *all*. If private efforts to deal with sin are unsuccessful, public exposure becomes necessary. The members of a church must be aware that the leaders take the sin seriously. Rejecting the sin, not the individual, is the aim. Nevertheless, to show compassion to a person unwilling to relinquish his or her sin is itself a way of taking sides against a holy and righteous God. When we refuse to confront, we fan the flames of self-deception and undermine the vitality of the Church.

When the Church speaks out about sin, on the other hand, in specific rather than general terms, it produces one of two opposite results. First, those who are the object of reproof may end their immoral behavior and seek forgiveness. Or they will go to more extreme measures to hide and protect their behavior. Reproof either entrenches or frees. For those who excuse their sin, confrontation may represent one of the steps to wholeness. It places a mirror of truth before those in self-deception. Whenever we face the truth, no matter how painful or revealing it is, our response determines our future spiritual vitality. As Proverbs says, "If anyone turns a deaf ear to the law, even his prayers are detestable" (Proverbs 28:9).

When a believer is living in obvious sin, therefore, we must judge him. If we refuse to face immorality, we provide sanctuary for it. And our unwillingness can open the door for other believers to sin.

4. Because God Commands Us To

God makes it clear in His Word that we are to judge. The case of sexual immorality in the Corinthian church is a good illustration. Paul said, "What business is it of mine to judge those outside the church? Are you not to judge those inside? God will judge those outside. 'Expel the wicked man from among you'" (1 Corinthians 5:12–13). In issues of doctrinal purity and morality, we are to be vigilant because God demands it.

I want to add a word of caution, however, because some people and ministries feel it is their special mandate from God to keep the Church pure. The problem arises when any of us becomes judge on a full-time basis. This is not necessary. More often it is done with an attitude of pride rather than with the hope of producing change. Dr. Michael

Brown calls these people "destructive critics" who, under the guise of strengthening the Church, can become guilty of gossip and slander. "Their hyper-suspicious, conspiracy-everywhere mentality," he says, "breeds bondage to fear and begets spiritual paralysis and inertia. This approach to gospel living poisons faith rather than produces faith."[2]

Afraid to Confront

Confronting another Christian is not about minor theological differences or dubious allegations. Rather, it must be about overt sin or rebellion.

During my high school years, I stayed close to the Lord. But during the last few weeks of school, I began to slip spiritually. My non-Christian friends were influencing me more than I was influencing them, and I began going to parties and drinking. Then a fellow Christian approached me in the high school print shop.

"Either get your life together," he said, "or stop calling yourself a Christian."

I was surprised at this admonition and resented him for judging me. So I brushed aside his comment and began to try to avoid him. This precious Christian who was once a valued friend was now someone I wanted to ignore. Yet deep inside I knew he was right. Weeks later I asked God to forgive me for friendship with the world, and I got back on track with Him.

The rebuke by my friend was an act of love. As a professing Christian, I was hurting the cause of Christ. And although I did not immediately accept my buddy's exhortation, it was not because I did not recognize the truth of what he said; it was because I had a rebellious heart. And later I was grateful he had not neglected his duty to confront me.

Given the rationales for confronting sin that we looked at in the last section, why is there still such a taboo within the Church against doing so? Maybe part of the problem is that we have not been taught how to confront in a spirit of love. In spite of the potential for misuse, judging sinful behavior must once again become a normal process within our churches.

Let's take a brief look at six reasons we have developed an aversion to confronting.

1. Skeletons of Our Own

The biggest reason many of us do not confront is that we have skeletons in our present or past. We may think it is best under these circumstances to simply live and let live. We are afraid to face others because we know our own sin is just as bad. In so doing, we selectively concentrate on the "softer" attributes of God's character like mercy, grace and peace.

2. Conflict Avoidance

A second reason we shirk from confrontation is that most of us prefer to avoid conflict. Life is more tranquil when we stay off hard issues. It is unsettling to think about or deal with sin. And many of us are too busy to get involved in someone else's life. It takes time and requires commitment.

3. Skewed Values

A third reason we do not confront is that our personal thinking and belief systems are messed up. We believe such rejoinders as "Who do you think you are to judge me?" and "What I do with my life is none of your business!" The world treats the confrontation of sin as immorality. The humanist says, "Don't cram your values down my throat!" But we need to recognize the source of the world's manipulative powers or else, in our desire to be fair and reasonable, we will begin to accept its moral mentality as normal and accept the values of this world.

4. Fear of Rejection

The fourth reason we are afraid to confront sin is that we fear rejection. It is naïve to think we will receive a warm reception when we challenge sin, but when confrontation occurs in a spirit of love, our chances of getting through are much greater. This does not mean, however, that our words will always bring a positive response. Many people who heard Jesus speak or received the benefit of His healing touch still did not make Him their Lord. "Even after Jesus had done all these miraculous signs in their presence, they still would not believe in him" (John 12:37).

5. Fear of Hurting Others

A fifth reason we do not judge is that we fear hurting someone's feelings. But it is a trap of the enemy to keep the Church from confronting error based on false compassion or misplaced sensitivity. We have become more sensitized to the feelings of those who have sinned than we are to God or others.

6. Preferring Peace at Any Price

A final reason we may avoid confrontation is to keep the peace. For many of us, unity has become an end in itself. Since confrontation is the opposite of harmony, and since confrontation almost always produces at least temporary disunity—and sometimes division—we avoid it. Yet if our reason for not judging sinful behavior is to preserve peace at any cost, it is placing our own interests above God's. We cannot knowingly ignore or approve sinful behavior and expect that it will not affect us in some way.

Our aim as the Church is not to manufacture unity at any price. Unity is a byproduct of living and interacting in right relationship with God and our fellow believers. Any kind of immorality tips the scales and throws our moral equilibrium off balance. Jesus said, "If you hold to my teaching, you are really my disciples" (John 8:31). The knowledge of the truth comes after we "hold to" His teaching. When our highest priority is to know truth, confrontation for the sake of truth takes on new meaning. Some Christians think they are preserving the "unity of the Spirit" (Ephesians 4:3), but we can preserve and nurture unity only in an atmosphere of obedience to God.

Don't Just Do It

The advertising slogan for an athletic footwear company has been *Just Do It!* And for some overweight Americans this is good advice. There is just one problem. You cannot get into physical shape overnight. It takes time to get out of shape, and it takes time (and commitment and a change of habit) to get into shape.

In the same way, we cannot expect immediate change from confronting moral error. I have heard some Christians say, "Well, at least I was willing to do it!" But that is not good enough. The way we confront sin, as we will see in the next chapter, is vital in determining whether the confrontation will produce positive results. We must confront in a way that provides the greatest opportunity for a successful outcome while not compromising the absoluteness of God's Word.

And we must be willing to offer help. The following advertisement appeared in the personal section of my local newspaper:

BiWCF, sick of shallow relationships? Intelligent, artistic, fun-loving and romantic, 26, ISO same for friendship. Kid-loving.

The writer of this ad offered the reader some information about herself. She is bisexual and in search of someone just like her. She also professes to be a Christian. Since as a follower of Christ I am struck by the moral incompatibility of bisexual behavior and adherence to the Christian faith, I cannot help wondering: What would happen if another believer confronted this 26-year-old about the inconsistency in her life? What if he or she agreed to help her find a godly counselor? Confrontation without the hope and help of recovery is like failing to throw a life preserver to someone who has just fallen off a cruise ship.

It is common for us to find all kinds of excuses for ignoring sensitive issues. We feel insecure approaching someone with more education or prominence, or someone who is a more mature Christian, or someone who knows the Bible better. Nevertheless, it makes no difference whether a brother or sister has more education, more knowledge of the Bible or has been a Christian all his or her life. The *need* for confrontation is not at issue. The *way* we do it is.

As we consider the importance of judging, therefore, it is important that we recognize how to do it correctly.

Peeling Off Labels

Propagandists, politicians and public relations professionals know the value of labels. A well-placed label can either build an otherwise tarnished image or destroy a reputation. Labels can immediately classify a person or evoke a particular emotion. While there are many good uses for labels as a method of classifying or ranking, there are also self-serving uses. Christians have been derided, for example, by such labels as *fundamentalist, narrow-minded* and *bigot.* Within some of our churches we employ labels for people willing to confront moral error. These include *negative, judgmental, legalist, antagonist, unmerciful, hardhearted* and *rigid.*

Those who oppose any form of judgment or exhortation usually do so for their own protection, preferring to stay "positive." They also cite Scripture passages in their defense. Paul's admonition, for example, for us to "examine everything carefully; hold fast to that which is good" (1 Thessalonians 5:21, NASB). But determining what is good calls for a value judgment. Was the apostle being negative or judgmental?

Another verse used to dissuade confrontation is Philippians 4:8: "Whatever is true, whatever is noble, whatever is right, whatever is pure, whatever is lovely, whatever is admirable—if anything is excellent or praiseworthy—think about such things." This verse has become a favorite of those who do not believe in confronting. "Let's not be negative," they say. "It's under the blood." But if this verse means we should think only about the positive we see in one another, the logical conclusion is that we should ignore sinful conduct and focus on the good.

God wants us to look for the good and encourage one another whenever we honestly can. His Word does not mean, however, that we turn the other way when we see sin. It would be easier if we were living in a perfect world, but we are not. We must deal with negative issues, and these are rarely pleasant.

If we use Philippians 4:8 as a shield to deflect criticism, we run into problems. Let's consider some axioms of the Christian faith and apply elements of this verse to them. Is it *true* that sinners are heading for eternal separation from God? Is it *honest* to say that Christ died a savage and humiliating death on the cross? Is it *right* to assume that those who reject Christ are His enemies? Is it *honorable* to report a teacher who is molesting young children? If we buy into the labels that discourage confrontation, we develop a distorted perception of God in general and of Christianity in particular.

One illustration of this distortion is the unwillingness of some ministers to teach on any "depressing" aspects of the Bible. One proponent of this "positive-only" doctrine believes that teaching about sin can be destructive. By preaching sin and judgment, he says, the Church "can be, quite accidentally and unintentionally but nevertheless a destructive influence in the human personality and human life." Sin and evil, he states, stem from "a hunger for self-worth." And salvation is simply the "deliverance from the fear of evil."

Suffice it to say that our problem with sin stems not from low self-esteem but from rebellion, and that the absence of self-esteem can never be the scapegoat for sin.

A Checklist for Discernment

Discernment, as we have seen, is a key for combating self-deception within ourselves and the Church. There are ten major reasons we struggle with discernment. Each of these can blind us from sin in our own lives or from immorality influencing our homes or churches. Before we confront someone else with moral error, as we will discover in the next chapter, it is necessary that our own motives be right.

Use the list below to check your own life before you face others with their behavior. As you review this list, ask yourself whether any of these statements apply to you. Ask the Holy Spirit to open your heart and understanding to any changes He may want to make in your life or ministry.

1. Am I inadequately grounded in God's Word?
2. Do I tend to live my spiritual life through other people?
3. Do I tend to judge by outward appearance?
4. Do I tend to judge by performance?
5. Do I misunderstand the relevance and importance of exhortation?
6. Do I tend to accept what someone says or does rather than check it against the Word of God?

7. Could sin be blocking my ability to see immorality as God sees it?
8. Is it possible that I have a false sense of salvation, including a verbal commitment to Christianity without an accompanying change in behavior?
9. Do I want to believe in people who sound sincere but who hold ideas or beliefs that contradict my own beliefs or experiences?
10. Am I unable to hear the prodding of the Holy Spirit because of "excess moral baggage"? This might be anger, bitterness or sin that I have left unresolved.

Chapter Highlights

- Discernment, or the capacity to discriminate or judge, can be nurtured through knowing God's Word, asking Him for help and making decisions to judge rightly.
- We are to judge within the Church for four reasons: our love for each other; our love for God; to deter sin; and because God tells us to.
- We are afraid to confront or judge sinful behavior for many reasons, but foremost is our misunderstanding of scriptural admonitions to do so in love and for the purpose of restoration.
- Most of us do not want someone else judging us when we get off track spiritually. It is common for those being judged to label their accusers as negative, legalistic or unmerciful.

Tearing Down
the Strongholds

Have nothing to do with the fruitless deeds of darkness, but rather expose them.

Ephesians 5:11

There are good and bad ways of fulfilling the ministry of criticism among Christians. . . . This ministry is important, for all who seek truth and wisdom take up from time to time with wrong ideas and need correction.

J. I. Packer

It was eight in the evening when Betty glanced nervously at the clock on her kitchen wall. Her husband was late again. The knot she felt in her stomach was nothing new. It was the way she felt every night. She had flashbacks of the time her husband, Dick, drove their Chevrolet through the garage door. Or the time the police had called. They were kind but firm when they brought Dick home. She promised the officers she would get help for her husband, but when she brought up the subject of his drinking, he flew into a rage. "I can handle a drink or two!" he yelled. He refused to see a counselor, declaring, "Only emotionally unstable people see shrinks!" He threatened to leave the church if she went to their pastor. "It's nobody's business but my own," he growled.

Year after year Betty worried about Dick and how his behavior might destroy their home. She fretted that one day he would hit an innocent pedestrian, collide with another car or kill himself. At times she blamed herself for not doing something. But after a while Betty stopped talking to Dick about his drinking. It was one of those areas in their marriage that was untouchable and seemingly impossible to resolve. *It never does any good,* Betty thought, *so why stir up more trouble for myself?*

Betty was facing the same dilemma we all experience at one time or another. How could she tactfully uncover the self-deception that was destroying her husband? She had to face questions like *What is my responsibility to God or my family?* and *How hard should I press the issue?* She wondered, *Should I leave the matter in God's hands? Doesn't confronting the problem only make it worse?*

Most of us prefer to adapt to the behavior of a deceived person than to face him or her. It was easier for Betty to facilitate Dick's problem out of sheer exhaustion and a desire to keep the peace. But God's Word says, "Don't hate your brother. Rebuke anyone who sins; don't let him get away with it, or you will be equally guilty" (Leviticus 19:17, TLB). God's message is clear: We are responsible for one another; we are indeed our brother's keeper. Betty was responsible to God, to her husband, to her family and to members of her community—each a potential victim of Dick's moral denial.

Confrontation: The Key to Wholeness

A theology of confrontation is not popular in most churches. Author Don Matzat points out, however, that when "correcting theology is not widely practiced, it creates an invitation to deception."[1] Some people think Betty will never accomplish anything positive by continuing to stand up to her husband, but will only make her life more miserable. To be sure, the easiest thing Betty can do is adapt to Dick's behavior. This would be a mistake. Loving confrontation, as we will see, is never easy. In most instances it takes more than a single conversation to bring about change. But whenever we approach others with the reality of their sin, we kick the props out from under them. Proverbs says, "He who conceals his sins does not prosper, but whoever confesses and renounces them finds mercy" (Proverbs 28:13). It is easier to forgive and to have mercy when we know that sin has been forsaken.

In some cases, to be honest, there never is change. But Betty cannot allow her husband to threaten or abuse her verbally into remaining silent. If Dick is not fulfilling his biblical mandate to be a loving husband, he is in disobedience to God. In such circumstances he is not thinking clearly.

If we "let sleeping dogs lie," those dogs cannot do any harm. But a *laissez-faire* approach can drive a person deeper into deception. We will never solve the problem of sin, either in ourselves or in others, by ignoring it. Confrontation is the bucket of cold water that often shocks a sinner back to reality.

Merritt McKeon is a forty-year-old Christian attorney living in southern California. For several years her husband abused her, emotionally and physically, before she finally left him, taking their three children. "My batterer started attending church after I left him," says McKeon, "and he was able to convince many church members that I was at fault for leaving him. He found support by either pretending to have converted to Christianity, or telling everyone what a devoted husband and father he was. He was able to do what I had not been able to do: get support from others."[2] For McKeon the ultimate form of confrontation came when she left an unhealthy and abusive environment.

While it is right spiritually to work toward restoration whenever possible, the sad reality is that it is not always possible. Jesus provides some tough instruction about moral confrontation when a fellow believer sins. "If [your brother] refuses to listen even to the church," He says, "treat him as you would a pagan or a tax collector" (Matthew 18:17). In other words, after we have approached a fellow believer properly with sin, if he ignores all attempts at reconciliation, he should be treated as an unbeliever.

Four Principles about Confrontation

In the last chapter we explored some of the reasons we avoid confronting sin in ourselves or others. In this chapter we will see how to go about confrontation in a righteous, biblical way. But first let me point out four important principles about confronting someone who has created his or her own version of the truth.

First, as we have seen, *it is the person confronted with his sin who is responsible for change.* No matter how noble our reasons, we cannot *force* anyone to see truth, nor can we change people. Like the prophets Samuel, Nathan and Gad, we are responsible only to challenge sin. Sometimes confrontation breeds a hardening of heart and resentment toward the one who has exposed the sin. Occasionally it produces repentance and change.

Nathan's meeting with King David is a classic illustration of a positive, life-producing encounter. The words of the prophet, an emotional parable containing powerful word pictures, got to the crux of David's sin and penetrated his heart. Unlike King Saul, David acknowledged his sin. He did not try to ignore, cover or belittle what he had done.

He repented of it. The confrontation jarred David back to reality.

The second principle we must understand is that *when we fail to face sin in others, it becomes our sin.* Charles Finney wrote,

> For anyone to see rebellion and not reprove it or lift his hand to oppose it is itself rebellion. So, if a man sees rebellion breaking out against God and does not oppose it or makes no effort to suppress it, he is himself a rebel. Your silence encouraged his sin.[3]

A friend of a woman from the ministry I used to work for was renting a room to a young Christian man. Before long the man, who had been through a divorce a year earlier, became more than a renter. They began to share the same bed. I said to my colleague, "You realize you now have a duty to speak with her." She agreed, and a week later met with her friend. The landlady acknowledged that what she was doing was wrong but employed the usual excuses to assuage her guilt. "I know God wants me to be happy," she said. "I'm not hurting anyone." Even though the woman, sad to say, did not change her ways, my friend had fulfilled her biblical responsibility.

Third, we must remember that *a change of heart does not reverse the lingering effects of a person's sin.* It is selfish to repent just so we can evade the results of what we have done. God wants us to forsake our sin because it violates the way He designed us. If He removes the effect of sin, the deterrent effect of His law will be weakened.

Fourth, *confrontation often produces separation and conflict.* When we confront sin, we open ourselves up to hurt and rejection. Confrontation can create a temporary separation or a long-term breach. Separation occurring within a family is extremely difficult, as Betty's story illustrates. She could try to cope with her husband's behavior by adapting, or risk being labeled meddling, picky or unsupportive. After Samuel made his final appeal to King Saul, he "did not see Saul again until the day of his death" (1 Samuel 15:35, NASB). Any healthy Christian relationship has an attendant mutual responsibility of fidelity to God and commitment to one another. Saul failed in his loyalty to God, which created the breach with Samuel.

Setting the Stage

The first question many of us ask, once we agree that confrontation is the biblical route to follow in a given situation, is, How do I get started? There are nine steps to follow.

The first and most important place to begin is with yourself. *Never face anyone else until you have examined your own heart.* This means you should run a diagnostic check of your motives. Are you considering confrontation to "set the record straight" or to prove how "righteous" you are? You must be above reproach. Before you approach another believer with his or her sin, be sure you have dealt with any anger, bitterness or jealousy hidden in your own heart.

Some of us are quick to point out fault whenever we see it. We are on the lookout for error—except within ourselves. Attempts to find fault with others can be a way to make ourselves appear more righteous. This can easily foster an attitude of self-righteousness instead. Hypocritical judgment rarely yields good fruit.

The second element in the preparation for confronting is this: *Make sure you have accurate information.* The story of the ten blind men who touched the elephant shows how easy it is to draw faulty conclusions. When we act on information that is wrong, incomplete or from a third party, we risk needless embarrassment and hurt. A quick examination of Matthew 18:16 makes clear when and how to involve others in the process. The checking and rechecking of facts is not necessarily gossip, although it can be if not handled with godly discretion. Always be sure you are acting on correct information and with the motivation to produce restoration.

Third, when confronting a fellow Christian, *do it in the name of the Lord.* It is easy to take any rejection personally without remembering that it is God's law and purposes, not ourselves, that have been violated.

As a fourth step, *prepare the facts.* Would you lead a Bible class for which you had not prepared? If you are meeting with someone deep in deception, facts are essential. Facts represent truth. Don't be general about the sin. A deceived person can talk his way out of nearly any kind of moral quagmire. And be ready to back your facts with God's Word.

Fifth, *prepare your heart beforehand.* When Queen Esther agreed to approach King Xerxes on behalf of the Jewish people, she asked Mordecai to "gather together all the Jews . . . and fast for me" (Esther 4:16). The Scripture also says that "the queen writhed in great anguish" (verse 4, NASB). She did not rush in to the king in a fit of anger and demand a change in his decree to destroy the Jews. Queen Esther knew the risks; she had the facts; she prepared her heart.

As a sixth and often overlooked element, *remember the importance of timing.* Esther knew what was at stake and chose the time wisely. Even after she approached Xerxes' throne, she did not reveal what was on her heart. When the king asked her to state her request, rather than blurt out her petition, she prudently invited him to a banquet. Later, when she delivered her appeal, the circumstances were in her favor. If a person is tired, emotionally distressed or preoccupied with other matters, wait. Plan adequate time to say what you need to say. Select a time that suits both parties. Be flexible to the other person's schedule and frame of mind.

Seventh, *select the location carefully.* If you are meeting with a spouse or family member, get away from the house. Choose a spot where noise, telephones or other interruptions will not hinder your conversation. Select a neutral spot like a park or restaurant. You may want to get into your car and drive a few miles away. A controlling person will tend to walk out during your meeting or try to control as much of the conversation as possible. By selecting a suitable location, you reduce his or her chances of controlling the meeting or trying to escape when it becomes uncomfortable.

The eighth ingredient is, *be sure you use discretion.* If possible, withhold the subject matter until your meeting. If the person pressures you to divulge the content of the conversation ahead of time, say, "There are several things that have been on my heart. May I share them with you?" The element of surprise gives the individual the chance to respond spontaneously. If you tip your hand in advance, it gives the person time to plan a rebuttal. But remember, it is not your purpose to secure a confession. You are merely stating the *fact* of the sin. The onus for dealing with the sin is on the other person's shoulders.

Generally you can interpret a quiet or thoughtful response from the other person as a positive sign. There may be times, however, when he or she will say, "What should I do?" or "Will you help me?" Be prepared to offer direction.

When I was seven, my parents discovered that I had stolen a five-cent Tootsie Roll. It would have been easy for my mother to say, "Son, don't ever do that again." She could have punished me or prayed with me, and I would have been glad to ask God to forgive me. She chose neither of these alternatives. The option she chose was to get involved. My mother drove me back to the market so I could confess my deed to the store manager and pay what I owed.

At times it is better to let a person face the consequences personally. It is tempting for us as parents to act on our children's behalf. This is seldom a wise choice. It is tempting to try to solve someone else's problem. Trust the Holy

Spirit to give you wisdom about how much you ought to get involved.

Finally, *the initial contact should take place one on one.* It is not fair to meet the other person with a small entourage! This is inappropriate and intimidating. Anyone who has been on the receiving end of correction should be sensitive to the other person. It is never easy to receive a rebuke. The degree to which you protect his or her integrity and reputation may determine the degree to which he or she hears God's loving call to forsake sin.

Special note: There are two exceptions to the solo rule. First, when you fear for your physical safety. Second, when a person's behavior has not changed after a previous one-on-one meeting. More on this in a minute.

When to Confront Sin

Uncovering sin is a solemn task that carries great responsibility. To expose sin in the wrong way or from the wrong motive is a serious matter. When you decide to expose sin publicly, it must be done within the local church. You accomplish little by venting the error to secular sources.

The apostle Paul said, "Have nothing to do with the fruitless deeds of darkness, but rather expose them" (Ephesians 5:11). Once we have confronted in private, we are to make the sin public only if the person persists in the behavior. An ample amount of time must be given for the reproof to take effect. If you reprove someone in spiritual authority, it is to be done on the basis of two or three witnesses (see 1 Timothy 5:19–20). If the person is intent on sinning, the matter must be taken to the elders within the church.

God's Word cautions us

> not to associate with any so-called brother if he should be an immoral person, or covetous, or an idolater, or a reviler, or a drunkard, or a swindler—not even to eat with such a

one. For what have I to do with judging outsiders? Do you not judge those who are within the church?

1 Corinthians 5:11–12, NASB

In many of our churches, however, we not only associate with "so-called brothers," but we allow their behavior to influence the weaker members of the Body of Christ. Here is the key distinction: Our relationships with the ungodly—those who do not profess Christ—are different from our relationships with those who proclaim Christ but act in an ungodly manner.

For new believers the discipleship process is crucial if we are to keep our churches above reproach. We may be tempted to call them "spiritually immature," and reason that it is better to let them continue in their sin until they see their own failure. Wouldn't we rather have them in the Church than out in the world? Surely a little exposure to the truth will lead to obedience. And I frequently hear the argument, "We must be merciful."

But to reverse this logic is to say that those who judge righteously are callous and unloving. God is both just *and* merciful. We must recognize that it is possible to maintain both attributes without compromise.

How to Confront Sin

By now you may have done some housecleaning of your own. You may be having second thoughts. You may even have confirmed your own rationale for bailing out. You may be reasoning, *It's really up to God*, or, *Let someone else do it.* This is a normal temptation, but forge ahead, until you have invested time in thought, prayer and perhaps fasting. It is always God's agenda and His will that we must place above our own reputation.

In general, confront in person. For some this is difficult, because personalities differ. A timid, quiet person has more difficulty confronting than an aggressive or assertive type. The timid personality is often more successful, however, because he or she approaches the person in a non-threatening manner. If you cannot meet face to face because of geography or schedule, make a phone call. As a last resort, write a letter.

How do you handle the knowledge of past sin? If a person has dealt with his or her sin, keep it confidential. Try to protect the reputation of a fellow believer whenever possible.

The degree of sin is a factor in how we approach a person in deception. "If an individual is ignorant," Charles Finney writes, "reproof should be more in the form of instruction. . . . You proceed very differently from what you would with a hardened sinner."[4] The more persistent a person is in sin, the harsher the rebuke.

What should you do during the encounter? Here are nine steps.

1. Intervene Early

Deal with sinful behavior early. By deferral we can lose a vital opportunity. Criminal law recognizes the importance of a fair and speedy trial (although it is rarely practiced). Similarly the certainty and speed of a confrontation will serve as a deterrent for further ungodly behavior.

The person who has sinned may think that what he or she has done is not so serious. If it was such a big deal, someone would have said something. Then, when we repeat sin, we become entrenched in it and it is harder to break free. It is like driving down a road that comes to a fork. If we select the proper road, we will reach our destination. But the farther we head down the wrong road, the more difficult it is to go back.

People who are in self-deception do not think straight. When we are living in sin, it is as if we have moral blinders on. We think only for the moment. Under such circumstances, we rarely consider the consequences of our actions. This is one reason moral intervention is so important. While it is crucial to confront soon after the immoral behavior, there are times when it is important not to act too early. In such instances, an overreaction can be counterproductive. A brief time buffer can give us the chance to gain our own composure when we might otherwise feel like blowing up.

2. Be Positive

Be as positive as you can without using flattery or manipulation. Communicate warmth, letting the person know you recognize his or her fine qualities. (At the same time, if you overemphasize the positive, the main point of your meeting may be lost.)

When we go on the offensive against sin it is never easy. It never should be. If you feel no anxiety, there is a good chance your motives are not pure. When the stage is set, don't blurt out your concerns. Be patient, natural and try to carry on a pleasant conversation in the beginning.

3. Relax and Be Direct

Be aware of your body language and posture. Though your body will be tense, try to relax during your opening remarks. Sit facing the other person. Concentrate on maintaining eye contact. Avoid fidgeting or playing with a pen or napkin. This lets the other person know you are serious. If your eyes wander or your head is down, these gestures may be misread as your own apprehension.

4. Control the Conversation

Maintain control by prefacing your comments with a statement like, "I have something very important to share with you. It's hard for me, so I would appreciate the chance to complete my thoughts." Interruptions can ruin what God wants to accomplish in a person's life.

5. Don't Use Notes

Don't take notes with you. Be sure you know beforehand what you want to say. Ask the Lord to help you organize your thoughts, remember what you need to say and articulate your concerns clearly. Why should you leave notes behind? The other person will feel intimidated or get the impression that this is an inquisition. Notes can also distract you and make it more difficult to keep eye contact.

6. Keep the Right Spirit

Remember that the rebuke comes from God through you. If you maintain the right spirit, you will get the point across. If you are attacked verbally, remain calm. It is common for people to become defensive and try to divert attention from themselves, sometimes to an unrelated problem in your own life. Be gentle but firm: "I'm willing to discuss that at another time, but it isn't the issue here." Don't get sidetracked. If the other person responds harshly, let it be because you are standing for righteousness, not because you have overreacted or communicated poorly.

7. Don't Reject the Other Person

Be sure you are expressing God's displeasure with sin, not your own personal rejection. Biblical confrontation is designed to produce change, but this does not mean we cut ourselves off from people who have sinned. Though Jesus never compromised sinful behavior, He spent much of His time with publicans and sinners.

It is worth taking a moment to explain the concept of separation from the world, because it is easily misunderstood. Christians today use the stories of the woman at the well and the woman caught in adultery in one of two ways. First, we may read them as Jesus' unwillingness to carry out the moral law. Or second, to emphasize His compassion for sinners, from which we deduce that all sinners are the same. Neither of these conclusions provides a complete picture. Though Jesus did not carry out the penalty of the law, He was not sanctioning the sin of these women. He was using the occasions to convey the state of each woman's heart. He used the moral law as a mirror to penetrate their blindness.

What makes the sins of Christians any different from that of unbelievers? Our degree of moral knowledge *and* our willingness to submit to it. The Christian who excuses his behavior, as we have seen, is in a far worse position than someone who has had little or no exposure to the truth.

8. Be Specific

Perhaps the most crucial component of the confrontational encounter is the need to be specific. You may assume that the other person knows what you mean. But deception may be blocking awareness of his or her spiritual condition. When you are specific, you leave little room for misunderstanding or confusion. Be direct and precise about sin. If you are unsure that the message is getting through, repeat it. Don't be afraid to ask if the other person understands.

9. Be Humble

Finally, if your heart is clean before the Lord and your attitude is right, you will exude humility. This does not mean you do not stand your ground. But nothing spoils the atmosphere of a confrontation more quickly than a self-righteous attitude. When we express the truth of God's Word, it never gives us a license to be proud.

Special Relations

The Bible instructs us not to "rebuke an older man harshly, but exhort him as if he were your father. Treat younger men as brothers, older women as mothers, and younger women as sisters, with absolute purity" (1 Timothy 5:1). The employee who confronts his supervisor must do so in a slightly different way than a wife would her husband.

Approaching a Christian Superior

There are few more complicated relationships in the Bible than David's with King Saul. David was not only Saul's son-in-law and servant, but his anointed successor. David's life serves as an example of how to approach a superior.

David and his men fled for their lives as Saul and three thousand of his chosen men chased them through the desert south of Jerusalem. When David found shelter in the recesses of a cave, Saul came in to relieve himself. The young man cut off a piece of the king's robe. Then, when Saul was far enough away, David called out to him, saying, "My lord the king!" (1 Samuel 24:8). He recognized Saul's superior position and rulership. When Saul turned around, the young man "bowed down and prostrated himself" (verse 8). David was assuring the king that he was not a threat. He expressed his past loyalty and commitment. He even went so far as to call Saul "my father" (verse 11).

What was Saul's response to David's confrontation? He wept, saying, "You are more righteous than I. . . . You have treated me well, but I have treated you badly" (verse 17).

For the moment David had accomplished his mission. His humble spirit melted the heart of the jealous and vengeful king.

When we face an elder, employer, minister or parent, we should offer recognition and respect for the positional disparity. At the same time, as Charles Finney pointed out, "No relations in life, or relative circumstances of the parties, take away the obligation of this duty. Whatever the relation, you are to reprove sin, and are bound to do it in the name of the Lord."[5]

A person in a position of power presents special difficulties. The greater the power or control, generally speaking, the harder it is to awaken the person's conscience to sin. There are good reasons for this. First, where there is power, pride is often present. Second, power or position creates detachment. There is a division between those who possess the power and those under the power. Third, positional or charismatic authority such as a visionary's is often equated in evangelical circles with God's presence. Fourth, the appetite for power is, for many, insatiable. Acknowledging sin is frequently seen as weakness or losing face. And fifth, the more power one has, the greater the opportunity to sin. And as one succumbs to sin, there is a greater need to cover the sin and protect one's position.

We are reluctant to face the sin of those holding office or power. For an employee it can cost a job. We cannot afford to ignore a Christian who is in sin, however, simply because he or she is influential. Does this mean we target those in leadership? No. Nor are we to be openly critical of others when we have neglected to search our own hearts. But God is no respecter of persons where sin is involved.

Complex Situations

It can be argued that *every* need to confront sin or error is complex. But some situations require a more careful approach. This is especially true when it comes to those in leadership.

It has been a common evangelical taboo to question, let alone "judge" or confront, a leader. Few are bold enough to do so, and those who do may be compared with Miriam and Aaron, whom God struck with leprosy for speaking out against Moses. It was not gross sin or deception, however, that Miriam and Aaron were murmuring about. Be wary of those who use such excuses to rationalize their position.

The first thing you should do, when you are aware of immorality in a leader, is to go directly to the person who has sinned. If this is unsuccessful, or if the leader of a large ministry, business or church is inaccessible, then go to those in authority over him or her.

But this may fail, for several reasons. A trustee may be afraid of or intimidated by the leader. Second, he may be in deception himself. Third, he may reason, falsely, that he is "protecting the Lord's anointed" (see 1 Chronicles 16:22). Those in authority often perpetuate this excuse to protect their position if they are controlling, or if they are trying to hide sinful behavior. This Scripture, they believe, validates their control.

Let's explore the biblical origin of this defense. There are two instances in God's Word in which David refused to lay a hand on King Saul, the Lord's anointed—1 Samuel 24:10 and 26:11. On both occasions David was so close to Saul that he could have taken his life. In the first account (the one we just looked at), David's men urged him on, saying, "This is the day the LORD spoke of when he said to you, 'I will give your enemy into your hands'" (1 Samuel 24:4). In the second account David's companion, Abishai, said, "Today God has delivered your enemy into your hands. Now let me pin him to the ground with one thrust of my spear . . ." (1 Samuel 26:8).

There is a big difference, however, between murdering the king, which David forbade, and questioning sinful conduct! It is a perversion of Scripture to use either of these passages as a shield against confronting the sin of those in authority.

We have an obligation to address sin when we become aware of it. If those in authority over a leader refuse correction, contact the denomination or higher authority structure, if one exists. Send a copy of your specific concerns in written form. This should include a brief outline of the problem. Beyond this, little else can be done without making the sin a public issue.

Approaching a Supervisor

The task of appealing to a Christian boss or supervisor is especially hard because it is difficult to separate the hierarchical relationship from the moral issues. Because the employee's job or status is at stake, the risk is greater.

Those who confront a Christian leader regarding illegal or unethical business practices, sexual advances, unfairness or mistreatment are heroes. Like the watchmen on the walls in Isaiah 62:6, they warn of impending calamity.

From the outset, communicate your loyalty as an employee. An employer, in order to muffle an employee, may attach labels like *divisive, troublemaking, malcontent* and *subversive* to soothe his or her conscience and make what is wrong appear right. One final note of caution: Do not discuss your employer's immoral behavior with your coworkers unless it relates directly to them. If you need counsel, it is best to go outside the workplace.

Final Words

There will be times your warning is ignored. How often, we may ask, should we confront? Samuel did not let Saul off the hook with a single encounter. He was tenacious! Matthew 18 makes plain that we are to disassociate from those unwilling to listen to godly moral correction. By distancing ourselves, we communicate abhorrence for behavior God detests. As we saw in the case of Merritt McKeon, whose husband was abusing her, separation is a form of confronting. Yet a breach in any relationship is reparable if we walk according to God's Word and His ways.

Is it fitting to present the Gospel to unsaved loved ones more than once? Of course. Similarly, if we care about each other, we will do everything possible to turn one another from the tragedy of sin. If we love our neighbor as Jesus commands, then genuine love demands openness.

The apostle Paul told the church in Ephesus to "[speak] the truth in love" (Ephesians 4:15). As you are faithful, you must trust the Holy Spirit to be faithful. Once you have done all you can, let Him do all He will. There are times you will feel like a failure. Remember, God desires even more than you do to restore your loved ones and friends. Rest in this truth and you will find freedom.

Chapter Highlights

- Confronting others with sin is often a costly exercise. Nevertheless, we are responsible for one another. We are our brother's keeper.
- Deal with sinful misconduct early. Do not wait until a person has accepted the behavior as normal.
- Always examine yourself before approaching someone else.
- We cannot change other people. We must give God's Spirit a chance to work when we present truth to an individual in error.

Breaking Free

A Case Study

This chapter is an interview with Jonathan Willis (not his real name) and his wife, Cynthia. (Their story is told briefly in chapter 6.) Jonathan is a doctor working in the Midwest, a graduate of a Christian college. Cynthia is a registered nurse, businesswoman and homemaker. They have two young children. Jonathan became involved emotionally and sexually with a nurse at the hospital.

In this conversation between Jonathan and me, he describes how the affair came about and what he learned in the process.

Can you describe what happened?

A lot went into the ultimate transgression—when lust became sin. I have thought about the groundwork that was laid by the enemy and me. It happened over a long period. It was exactly what James 1:15 says: Lust gave birth to sin. I worked progressively from covert peeking at swimsuit issues of *Sports Illustrated* to smut magazines. This led into renting explicit R-rated and then X-rated videos. It was a habit, a conscious decision, but it was as addicting as alcohol or drugs.

The process also included fantasy. You can never satisfy lust. There are only intermittent satisfactions. You progress and it keeps a grip on you, which grows tighter. You don't necessarily feel out of control or controlled by it, but you *are* out of control.

The fantasy is what led to the actual transgression. It became part of the video imagination process.

Do you believe the videos created unrealistic expectations or hunger that you could not satisfy in a legitimate way?

The videos created a craving for something new, something unusual. It's the true wrong side of seeking after pleasure. God created us to have pleasure, to enjoy good tastes. But to pursue newness, in which variation is the hope, is wrong. What you're hoping for is more thrill, but this is not a conscious thought. If you think it through consciously, your mind is logical enough to say no. But the driving thought that rides under the surface of your logical, decision-making process influences your decisions.

What were some of the events or circumstances that led up to the adultery?

Early on, as a medical resident, I was almost devastated by what might be awaiting me. I had great anxiety. I slept rarely. The stress was numbing. As a resident you are beaten down. You do not develop confidence.

After two years went by, I began to relax. But the setting of a large medical center presented some problems. I was there all night on call. Many nights I wasn't doing anything—not doing cases, not seeing patients, getting only occasional phone calls. I was simply available. There were often women around who were not busy.

In any institution, even among Christians, you find people willing to have an affair. In this hospital was a woman brazen enough to let it be known. She was very unhappy with her marriage and was looking for a resident. She was involved in lust-producing activities. She and her spouse were into X-rated movies. She was a dirty storyteller in the OR. She would solicit the affection and attention of men. She made it a point to get to know me. Unfortunately she fit neatly into my fantasy and I was too willing to pay attention.

But for four weeks I resisted having sexual intercourse. It was some vague sense of a standard I needed to maintain. I didn't want to transgress what would be wrong physically. Yet during that time—and we met repeatedly—there was a lot of oral sex. A relationship began to develop. She fed my new fantasy. She was feeding my ego. She was building up my perception of myself. I needed that.

Was there anything that your wife did or did not do to provide encouragement or acceptance?

Cynthia struggles with this question. She often wonders how she contributed to my adulterous affair. The first thing I recognized in the beginning of my relationship with Cynthia is that I was very comfortable with her. It dawned on me one day that she was the one person I could really be myself with. I didn't have to think about how she responded to me. I just knew she looked at me with high regard. That was comfortable. If she had tried overtly to feed my confidence, I probably would have rejected it.

So the answer is no. The solution had to lie in another area.

How would you explain the direction your actions took, then?

I'm heading toward two different points. One was the overt, adulterous sin. It was clearly based on an opportunity to build up fantasy and continue that as a physical relationship. The other was the ego-emotional relationship, which actually became more difficult to break. A month into it, the relationship gave me the basis, at least within my mind, to go ahead physically.

I find Proverbs 7:7 very poignant. It says that "a youth who lacked judgment" went off with the harlot. If you don't have God's Word within your heart to protect you, your judgment will be severely lacking. And mine was.

I assumed the woman was using birth control, but she wasn't. After four more weeks she became pregnant. It made it horrible. It was like the worst monster of my nightmares coming true.

It was another four weeks before it became apparent to Cynthia that something was wrong. My behavior was different. Another doctor at work said, "Dr. Willis, you look like you're under severe stress." Physically and emotionally I felt normal, so this was like cold water in the face.

So your wife was aware that something was not right, and some of your colleagues were at least partially aware that something was going on. You knew that what you were doing didn't measure up to your belief system. What was happening inside you? What were you saying to yourself? How were you justifying what was going on?

I didn't think about it. I didn't evaluate it. My judgment was turned off.

You're a thinker. It must have been a difficult process to turn off.

No. It wasn't at all. That's the frightening part of it. It was easy. It occurred over a long period. This doesn't happen to somebody who decides correctly in his heart at every level most of his adult life. This is a step-by-step process. In almost imperceptible ways you make choices against your beliefs.

How do you do this?

You don't do anything more than live for the moment. I was closing off any outside or peripheral thoughts. I did not go through the normal process of planning, as most of us do. I would just go into my day and it would meet me. There was no need to think beyond the next two minutes.

When you went home at night, were you the same or different?

I was different. As time went on, it became easier. I was closing off my thought processes or consciousness. I was simply numb. I wasn't thinking. I was mechanical. I was not friendly or warm, not approachable. My sleep was not restful. I was tired all the time. And I was much more distant in my conversation. Cynthia didn't know how to broach the problem. Within her was a sense of denial.

One misconception I had concerning all this is a restraint I did *not* find in myself. If I had walked into a store and seen something I liked but didn't have the money to pay for it, and I had picked it up and put it into my pocket and walked out the door, I would have felt immensely guilty. It's not something I've ever done, nor would I ever imagine myself doing that. If I *were* to do that, the guilt would crush me. I would have to confess to keep from feeling so bad.

We think that's going to happen with any temptation. But it doesn't. That was the restraint I looked for but didn't find. It will not keep you from sinning. But we think it will.

You're saying you don't think your conscience was helping you through this process?

Right. We expect it to, but sometimes it doesn't. Over the year that I had the affair, I experienced contriteness—definite times of repentance. But I expected an overwhelming sense of shame that so aroused me to righteousness that I would stop what I was doing. It didn't happen. There's no question it was worn down through my activities.

I wish I could describe the blackness, the despair, the sense of separation from anything good. Those last four weeks I would wake up at three in the morning with an overwhelming sense of being lost, of hopelessness. I presume the source was a merciful God saying, "I love you too much to let you go on. I'm going to do what's necessary to get your attention."

You see, you have this strange, perverted hope that everything is going to be O.K. How could something so good be so wrong? You can easily understand why somebody puts a needle into his vein and shoots something into it. The thrill—the rush—excuses the bad feelings that eventually come. It's as if the Lord said to me, "I'm going to turn My back on you. You have abused your relationship with Me."

Yet throughout this whole time I still talked like a Christian. All the while—this is really disturbing—I maintained active participation at church. I always had the sense that going to church was the right thing to do. You can be doing things that are wrong, yet doing many right things, too. They feel right, and your mind says they *are* right and will bear fruit. If you've worked in yourself good habits of parenting, you're still a good parent. That doesn't stop. But it gives you false feedback. It says, "I'm not so bad."

But eventually I arrived at an emotional and mental state of unhealth. This was before Cynthia had the courage to confront me. I married a courageous woman who persisted, in the face of horrible things, to do what was right.

Throughout all of this, I would still sit down with my Bible and read. I would still pray. I had a very consistent time of prayer on my way in to work. I take no credit for that. It was habit. There was no goodness within me. I wasn't trying to counteract the sin I was committing. The conscience does not permit foolishness. I mean, we don't consider it foolish; otherwise we would stop doing it. It clearly describes why alcoholics, drug addicts or gamblers do what they do. They do not think about the future.

I did not have a full sense of the hurt or consequences of my actions. We expect a right awakening. The mind plays these endless games of justification. It hides us from evaluation—leading us away from thinking about it and being examined. You know that the examination process will reveal areas that need to change. They will hurt and be painful.

What about sex within your marriage? Was it any different?

It was much less. This all happened immediately after our second child was born. Cynthia blames herself strongly for some of this. She had not been available to me sexually. But this was really not part of my decision-making process. By the time she could have sex again, I was at the worst part of the other relationship. I was quick to anger because the stress was building inside me. I suddenly found myself yelling at the kids. I would get violent toward the dog and beat her mercilessly. I realize none of this is complimentary of me. I abused that dog. I would look up and see the shock on Cynthia's face. It was as if a veil covered my mind.

Were you transferring your guilt to appease your conscience?

Sure. The emotional overlay was now dictating to me. I didn't want to do non-Christian things, and non-Christian things included divorce. Yet what was occurring was also a want and a desire. These two were rapidly becoming incompatible.

What about your emotions?

I was very involved emotionally. If I could have thought rationally, based on the truth in God's Word, I would have stopped the adultery and done whatever it took to restore my marriage.

What would you have done if someone had confronted you?

I would have been shocked that anyone would address the issue. My conscious thought processes were narrow. I still thought I was doing O.K. I could still maintain superficial relationships.

What finally happened?

Cynthia figured out what was going on. I came home late one night totally exhausted. She came into the bedroom at two in the morning and confronted me. I confessed and went back to sleep. She left in the car, distraught. I woke up an hour later in fear. I realized Cynthia could kill herself. That was when I got scared.

We think that, when faced with the wrath of God, we're going to be afraid. I think Judgment Day is going to be full of very angry people. They will be angry at God. Hell is developing in people the moment they start making selfish decisions.

Once I realized I could lose the most precious thing in my life, I began thinking. The fear galvanized me. Now my world was really coming apart. The affair was costing me more than I was willing to pay.

How did Cynthia deal with the problem?

She met with the pastor and his wife that morning. He was very helpful, very skilled. He had handled these situations many times. He committed himself to us.

Was there any sense of embarrassment on your part?

Very much. This was the first time I had to admit I was spiritually unsound. I could no longer ever be good in the pastor's eyes. I had to go through the process of admitting what I had done. For the first time I saw an outside cost to this. I could never maintain the appearance of having it all together in that church again.

Was there any sense of relief?

There was sense of hope at first. I could say, "This is going to work." I didn't feel now that I was losing. The perception I had was that it was going to be easy. It was workable. It was just a matter of doing it. The pastor shared with us about another couple, and that husband finally said, "Why do we have to go through all this stuff? Why can't we just get on with living?" I thought, *That's exactly what I'm saying.* You want to say, "When is this going to end?" Finally Cynthia and I began telling each other what we appreciated about one another.

But as a few weeks went by, I became incredibly depressed. I almost felt that life wasn't worth living. I still wanted the other relationship. The ugliness of self-confidence and ego was now gripping me. I could have cared less about the sexual relationship. The last thing I wanted to do was see an X-rated video or look at a *Playboy.* I wanted to run from those things. I thought, *If I don't do those bad things, it may excuse other bad things.* It's like when you're faced with having to do the taxes, it becomes easy to clean up the backyard. I probably lost 20–25 pounds. I was dying to a relationship.

One of the consistent things people were telling me was, "Stop seeing this woman. Do not have any input from her at all." But I couldn't maintain that. It seemed clear to me that to come out of the depression simply took hearing her voice. So I spoke with her on the phone. It was just like a new needle in the arm.

The woman was a master of deceit, a very evil person. I don't say this to excuse my sin. Yet she was a professing Christian. I was like an ox going to the slaughter, a deer captured by the fowler's snare. I was caught up with this new desire to talk with her. This was after the confrontation with Cynthia, after weekly counseling sessions. I had no idea how to break the relationship off.

Cynthia had people praying coast to coast. She talked to anybody we knew, called them up, explained briefly and said, "Please pray for Jonathan."

Did that irritate you?

Yes. As more people find out, you want to cover it up. You want to crawl back under the rock. But people were praying very effectively.

The other thing that pulled me out of the relationship was that I was still in fellowship, still in a small group class. I was also trying to stay in the Word, although I was starting to find it difficult. I knew it to be a source of life. I hoped it would be the solution.

It wasn't. None of these individually provided the answer. Neither confrontation, church, the Word, confession, tears or remorse was enough. All of it together definitely helped.

What did make a difference?

One pivotal point was an experience I had in a little sailboat I owned. I was out sailing while Cynthia and the kids were on the grassy shore. I was really dealing with the question, *Am I going to continue with this marriage?* Before this point I would counter that question mentally with *Christians aren't supposed to get divorced.*

Then my son came running down the shore. That little boy means a lot. I saw his joy. I saw him with his mom. It was right. It was goodness. I knew I could always choose for my little boy. I could not justify his being raised by this other woman, even though she had tried to talk me into that. I was finally able to think it through. My decision was, *I will not be the one who chooses divorce.*

Then Cynthia called me at the hospital one night, obviously distraught. She wanted to settle this once and for all.

She presented me with the fact that this woman, who had been pregnant, had had an abortion. I had suspected it. Now the lights were on. I knew what Cynthia told me was true. It was that information that shattered the image I had of the woman. Now she could never have credibility in my mind. I knew I could turn my back on the relationship.

It was a necessary key leading to restoration. Cynthia made it absolute. I had to choose.

How were you able to turn away from your wife so easily?

One thing that gave me the capacity to turn away from Cynthia was that I had begun to turn from her in my mind. It was easy to be critical. Yet three weeks before the affair, I was praying, *Lord, work on my marriage.* I wanted to be closer to my wife. I wanted us to have a good marriage and a good home. Now my attitude toward her was one of mild contempt. I wasn't conscious of it; I just did it.

How has Cynthia been affected by your decisions?

She looks at herself very critically. When I see this most beloved person do this to herself, it really makes me evaluate what I did wrong. Now I ask myself, *Is there anything I do that affects her, that doesn't build her up?*

What is the hardest part of the rebuilding process?

Trust. It isn't just that the Lord fills a person with trust. I need to do everything *I* can. I want to give the appearance of being trustworthy. You can't practice at home what you don't do at work or elsewhere. Every single day, every single moment, I need to think through where I might compromise Cynthia's trust in relationships with other women. If Cynthia is not present, I practice her presence. Would she understand my putting my arm around this woman? If not, I don't do it.

What would you say to someone who reads this and says, "I'd never let that happen to me"?

Unless somebody is working actively *not* to have it happen, he is very vulnerable. We are all vulnerable. Unless you believe you are capable of having some gross sin come into your life, you will fall. What makes you weak is ignorance and persisting in that ignorance. You can say, "I am not vulnerable," but then you are ignorant to your own pride. An individual who says, "Under the right circumstances that could happen to me," is far more realistic. It doesn't have to be a naked woman. It can be in any other area.

Is it worth the effort for Christians to confront sin?

God uses people. He uses His Word and He answers prayer. We can't see the spiritual battle. When you walk up to someone and say, "You need to know Jesus," it doesn't make a difference right then. Nevertheless, you have planted a seed.

What advice do you have for a husband who fell?

Be patient with yourself. And don't do anything that would harm this fragile creature. Don't respond to defend yourself. You don't deserve your kids, your wife or your home.

Love is choosing the other person's highest good above your own. Do that. It's a choice, not a feeling. The feeling will come afterward. Love her practically. Do the dishes. Don't complain. Do whatever you can to relieve the normal stress that families have. Be the super husband, the super dad, without pride.

What counsel would you give to a wife struggling to forgive her husband? How do you let go of the pain, the past, the hurt?

Hope is crushed along with trust. So if I could plant a thought in the heart of every woman who went through what Cynthia did, it would be, *Try to look for Christ in your husband.* He is God's gift to you, no matter what horrible thing he's done to you. He is incomplete, yet he is Christ's best for you. Don't look at all the deficiencies. Look at what Christ can be through this man in your life and the life of your family. With that perspective, I think a wife can have hope.

Both husband and wife need to guard themselves against using little things to hurt one another. In every way possible, try to do what's right in the marriage. Be kind. Say, "I love you," and mean it. Think about what you are saying. Do you really mean that? Make that choice inside.

What is Cynthia feeling now that you are back together?

It takes just one thought to trigger hurt from the past. There will be days that are just a dream. Other days she will feel extreme anger, depression or despair. She must look at the positive progress we're making. It's important to bring out the memories that are good.

What spiritual lessons have you learned?

When you go through this kind of muck and can still feel God's presence, it's so good! God spoke very clearly to me through Psalm 91, giving me hope that He is my Deliverer. None of this could have taken place without God. He came down from the mountain and found His lost sheep, black as he was. That's a sense of God's commitment to me that I never want to lose sight of. He will see me through the trials of life. If He is with us when we are in sin, how much more when we are walking with Him?

Notes

Chapter 1: Nothing but the Truth

. 1. Quoted in Cal Thomas, *The Death of Ethics in America* (Waco, Tex.: Word, 1988), p. 145.

2. Cited in *Pentecostal Evangel*, July 10, 1994, p. 28.

3. Cited in *Pentecostal Evangel*, November 29, 1992, p. 24.

Chapter 2: Fighting the Mermaid Syndrome

1. Cited in "The Whoopee Monster," *Newsweek*, March 8, 1993, p. 56.

2. Cited in "Study: Sex Activity, Grades Unrelated," *Spokesman-Review*, May 12, 1994.

3. Cited in "Chuck Colson: Challenging the Church to Be a Light in a Dark World," *Ministries Today*, March/April 1993, p. 51.

4. Cited in "Abortion: Common at Christian Colleges," *Christianity Today*, July 14, 1989, p. 42.

5. "Women and the Churches," *Newsweek*, February 20, 1989, p. 38.

6. George Barna, *The Future of the American Family* (Moody, 1993), pp. 81–82, 187.

7. Glenn Tinder, "Can We Be Good without God?", *Atlantic Monthly*, December 1989, p. 69.

8. Charles H. Colson, *The God of Stones & Spiders* (Crossway, 1990), p. 153.

9. J. Oswald Sanders, *The Incomparable Christ* (Moody, 1971), p. 121.

10. Gordon MacDonald, "True Confessions," *Discipleship Journal*, 50, 1989, p. 9.

11. Zane Hodges, *Absolutely Free* (Zondervan, 1989), pp. 144–145.

12. Quoted in Bonhoeffer, *The Cost of Discipleship* (Collier, 1963), pp. 55, 57.

Chapter 3: Having It Our Way

1. Quoted in Robin Eastern, "Christian Morals," *Spokesman-Review*, January 11, 1997.

243

2. George Will, "A Trickle-Down Culture," *Newsweek*, December 13, 1993, p. 84.

3. John Leo, "Divorce—Society's Accepted Ailment," *Spokesman-Review*, September 24, 1994.

4. Joseph Califano, "Doctors Can't Cure Social Ills," *Spokesman-Review*, February 11, 1995.

5. Norman Lear, "Bottom Line Becomes a Bad Ethic," *Los Angeles Times*, n.d.

6. Quoted in Bruce McCabe, "Do Kids Show Signs of Moral Illiteracy?", *Spokesman-Review*, December 20, 1993.

7. Phil Rosenthal, "Too Much Blame Is Being Spread Around," *Spokesman-Review*, October 27, 1993.

8. Scott Montgomery, "The Buck Stops . . . There," *Spokesman-Review*, December 14, 1994.

9. Karl Menninger, *Whatever Became of Sin?* (New York: Hawthorn, 1973), p. 177.

Chapter 4: Excuses: Betraying the Truth

1. "Morality Takes a Beating in Hurricane Aftermath," *Seattle Times*, January 17, 1993.

2. Elizabeth Glieck, "Three Kids, One Death," *Time*, December 2, 1996, pp. 69–70.

3. Margaret Carlson, "Children without Souls," *Time*, December 2, 1996, p. 70.

4. *National & International Religion Report*, November 30, 1992.

5. "Was It Good for Us?", *U.S. News & World Report*, May 19, 1997, p. 60.

6. "If He Could Make It Here," *Newsweek*, December 21, 1992, p. 57.

7. Michelle Malkin, "Why Ellen Is Tolerable but Heather's Moms Aren't," *Seattle Times*, April 15, 1997.

8. "Researchers Can't Confirm Genetic Link to Alcoholism," *Los Angeles Daily News*, April 29, 1990.

9. "What They Preach . . .", *Washington Post*, October 17, 1993.

10. Wray Herbert, "Politics and Biology," *U.S. News & World Report*, April 21, 1997, pp. 77–78.

11. William Glasser, *Reality Therapy* (New York: Harper & Row, 1974), p. 182.

12. Quoted in Jim and Phyllis Alsdurf, "The Generic Disease," *Christianity Today*, December 9, 1988, p. 33.

13. "Toxic Parents, Perennial Kids: It's Time for Adult Children to Grow Up," *Ute Reader*, November/December 1990, pp. 61–62.

14. Quoted in *AFA Journal*, August 1993, p. 11.

15. "Christians Spar at Harvard," *Time*, March 16, 1992, p. 49.

16. "40 Churches Defy 'Chastity' Amendment," *Washington Post*, May 16, 1997.

17. Roper Limobus Survey, commissioned by High Adventure Ministries, Simi Valley, Calif., April 1990.

18. Allan Bloom, *The Closing of the American Mind* (New York: Simon & Schuster, 1987), pp. 119–120.

19. John P. Robinson, "I Love My TV," *American Demographics,* September 1990, p. 24.

20. Victor Strasburger, "My Turn: Tuning In to Teenagers," *Newsweek,* May 19, 1997, p. 18.

21. Rolf Zettersten, "Ted Bundy: A Fatal Addiction," *Focus on the Family,* March 1989, p. 23.

22. C. Wright Mills, *The Sociological Imagination* (New York: Oxford, 1959), p. 170.

23. Quoted in Joel Feinberg, *Reason and Responsibility* (Belmont, Calif.: Wadsworth, 1981), pp. 419, 421.

24. "The Jessica Hahn Story," *Playboy,* July 1987, Part 1, p. 80.

25. Charles G. Finney, *Principles of Victory* (Minneapolis: Bethany, 1981), p. 89.

26. Michael Saks, *Social Psychology and its Implications* (New York: Harper & Row, 1988), p. 229.

Chapter 5: The Antidote to Moral Meltdown

1. Robertson McQuilkin, *Biblical Ethics* (Wheaton, Ill.: Tyndale, 1989), p. 52.

2. Ralph Kinney Bennett, "How Honest Are We?", *Reader's Digest,* December 1995, pp. 49–55.

3. Daniel R. Levine, "Cheating in Our Schools: A National Scandal," *Reader's Digest,* October 1995, pp. 65–70.

4. Peter Kim and James Patterson, *The Day America Told the Truth* (New York: Plume, 1992), pp. 6, 8.

5. "Our Sexual Revolution Casualties Grow," *Los Angeles Daily News,* June 12, 1989.

6. Debra Koenig, "Perspectives," *Newsweek,* May 10, 1993, p. 17.

7. "Unfaithfulness, Cervical Cancer Tied," *Spokesman-Review,* August 7, 1996.

8. John J. DiIulio Jr., "Deadly Divorce," *National Review,* April 7, 1997, pp. 39–40.

9. Del Jones, "Doing the Wrong Thing," *USA Today,* April 4–6, 1997.

10. Ibid.

11. Werner Heisenburg, *Across the Frontiers* (New York: Harper & Row, 1974), p. 213.

12. Quoted in Feinberg, *Reason,* p. 347.

13. R. J. Rushdoony, *Institutes of Biblical Law* (Philipsburg, N.J.: Presbyterian and Reformed Publishing, 1973), p. 4.

14. Kent Wilson, "Holiness: Now and to Eternity," *Discipleship Journal,* 49, 1989, p. 26.

15. Kim and Patterson, *America,* pp. 27, 34.

16. Cited in *Pentecostal Evangel,* July 10, 1994, p. 28.

17. Quoted in John Lofton, "The War on Absolutes," *Chalcedon Report,* October 1989, p. 11.

18. Herbert Schlossberg, *Idols for Destruction* (Nashville: Nelson, 1983), p. 275.

19. Ravi Zacharias, *Deliver Us from Evil* (Dallas: Word, 1996), p. 93.

20. Menninger, *Sin,* p. 198.

21. Charles G. Finney, *Lectures to Professing Christians* (Concord, Tenn.: Denton, 1928), p. 80.

22. Menninger, *Sin,* p. 180.

23. Schlossberg, *Idols,* p. 268.

Chapter 6: The Symptoms of Compromise

1. Michelle Green, "Control Freaks," *Self,* July 1992, p. 117.

2. Quoted in M. Scott Peck, *People of the Lie* (Simon & Schuster, 1983), p. 81.

3. Ibid., p. 255.

Chapter 7: Black Holes and Moral Tar Pits

1. Peck, *Lie,* pp. 78, 82.

2. Bonhoeffer, *Discipleship,* p. 75.

3. George Otis Jr., *The God They Never Knew* (Lynnwood, Wash.: Sentinel, 1978), p. 20.

4. Quoted in Robert Warren Cromey, "Celebrate and Guide Sexuality," *Los Angeles Times,* May 31, 1991.

5. Stephanie Brommer, "Debate Continues Over Sex Report," *Los Angeles Daily News,* June 15, 1991, p. 14.

6. Quoted in Kurt Back, et al., *Social Psychology* (New York: Wiley & Sons, 1977), p. 184.

Chapter 8: The Father of Lies

1. Jessie Penn-Lewis, *War on the Saints* (Kent, England: Diasozo Trust, 1973), p. 100.

2. Lance Morrow, "Evil," *Time,* June 10, 1991, p. 51.

3. Schlossberg, *Idols,* p. 6.

4. Penn-Lewis, *War,* p. 106.

5. C. S. Lewis, *The Screwtape Letters* (New York: Bantam, 1982), p. 69.

6. Dean Sherman, *Spiritual Warfare for Every Believer* (Seattle: YWAM, 1990), p. 130.

7. Gordon MacDonald, *Rebuilding Your Broken World* (Nashville: Nelson, 1988), p. 54.

8. "Republican Version of Family Values Does Not Address Deepest Concerns," *Spokesman-Review,* August 25, 1992.

9. Quoted in Neil Hickey, "How Much Violence?", *TV Guide,* August 22–28, 1992, p. 11.

10. Peter Marshall and David Manuel, *The Light and the Glory* (Grand Rapids: Fleming H. Revell, 1977), pp. 200–201.

11. Patricia McLaughlin, "Imitation Status Symbols," *Los Angeles Daily News*, April 6, 1989.

12. Lewis, *Screwtape*, p. 27.

Chapter 9: Olber's Paradox

1. Quoted in "Beware of the Satanic Setup," *The Christian Chronicle*, December 1991, p. 8.

2. Jamie Buckingham, "Last Word: Philistines and the Media," *Charisma*, January 1992, p. 90.

3. Andrew Young, quoted in interview, *Modern Maturity*, March/April 1997, p. 59.

4. Buckingham, "Philistines," p. 90.

5. "The Independence Myth," *Christianity Today*, January 15, 1990, p. 32.

6. David Wilkerson, *Set the Trumpet to Thy Mouth* (Lindale, Tex.: World Challenge, 1985), p. 45.

7. Oswald Chambers, *My Utmost for His Highest* (New York: Dodd, Mead, 1935), p. 18.

8. Juan Carlos Ortiz, *Disciple* (Carol Stream, Ill.: Creation House, 1975), p. 43.

9. Don Basham, *True and False Prophets* (Grand Rapids: Chosen, 1986), p. 60.

Chapter 10: Pushing the Envelope

1. "In Defense of the Little White Lie," *Redbook*, July 1995, p. 33.

2. "Finders, Keepers: Honesty, A Lost Policy," *Money*, August 1994.

3. Francis Schaeffer, *The Great Evangelical Disaster* (Westchester, Ill.: Crossway, 1984), p. 63.

4. McQuilkin, *Ethics*, p. 377.

Chapter 11: Removing the Scales

1. David Wilkerson, "The Persecution of the Righteous," newsletter, April 13, 1987, p. 4.

2. Michael L. Brown, *Let No One Deceive You* (Shippensburg, Pa.: Destiny Image, 1997), p. 55.

Chapter 12: Tearing Down the Strongholds

1. Don Matzat, *Inner Healing: Deliverance or Deception?* (Eugene, Ore.: Harvest House, 1987), p. 36.

2. Merritt McKeon, *Stop Domestic Violence* (New York: St. Martin's, 1997), p. 99.

3. Charles G. Finney, *Lectures*, p. 15.

4. Ibid., pp. 19–20.

5. Ibid., p. 19.

Selected Bibliography

Back, Kurt, et al. *Social Psychology*. New York: Wiley & Sons, 1977.

Barna, George. *The Future of the American Family*. Chicago: Moody, 1993.

Basham, Don. *True and False Prophets*. Grand Rapids: Chosen, 1986.

Bellah, Robert. *Habits of the Heart*. New York: Harper & Row, 1985.

Bloom, Allan. *The Closing of the American Mind*. New York: Simon & Schuster, 1987.

Bok, Sissela. *Lying: Moral Choice in Public and Private Life*. New York: Vintage, 1978.

Bonhoeffer, Dietrich. *The Cost of Discipleship*. New York: Collier, 1963.

Carter, Stephen L. *The Culture of Disbelief*. New York: Anchor, 1993.

Colson, Charles L. *Against the Night*. Ann Arbor: Vine, 1989.

Finney, Charles G. *Lectures to Professing Christians*. Concord, Tenn.: Denton, 1928.

Glasser, William. *Reality Therapy*. New York: Harper & Row, 1974.

Kim, Peter and James Patterson. *The Day America Told the Truth*. New York: Plume, 1992.

Lewis, C. S. *Mere Christianity*. New York: Macmillan, 1952.

_____. *The Screwtape Letters*. New York: Bantam, 1982.

MacDonald, Gordon. *Rebuilding Your Broken World*. Nashville: Nelson, 1988.

Manuel, David and Peter Marshall. *The Light and the Glory*. Grand Rapids: Fleming H. Revell, 1977.

McQuilkin, Robertson. *Biblical Ethics*. Wheaton, Ill.: Tyndale, 1989.

Menninger, Karl. *Whatever Became of Sin?* New York: Hawthorn Books, 1973.

Neuhaus, Richard John. *The Naked Public Square*. Grand Rapids: Eerdmans, 1984.

Ortiz, Juan Carlos. *Disciple*. Carol Stream, Ill.: Creation House, 1975.

Peck, M. Scott. *People of the Lie*. New York: Simon & Schuster, 1983.

Penn-Lewis, Jessie. *War on the Saints*. Kent, England: Diasozo Trust, 1973.

Selected Bibliography

Rushdoony, R. J. *Institutes of Biblical Law.* Philipsburg, N.J.: Presbyterian and Reformed Publishing, 1973.

Schaeffer, Francis A. *The Great Evangelical Disaster.* Westchester, Ill.: Crossway, 1984.

Sherman, Dean. *Spiritual Warfare for Every Believer.* Seattle: YWAM, 1990.

Thomas, Cal. *The Death of Ethics in America.* Waco, Tex.: Word, 1988.

Wilkerson, David. *Set the Trumpet to Thy Mouth.* Lindale, Tex.: World Challenge, 1985.

Index

Don Otis has worked for Christian radio and television in the U.S. and the Middle East, and has served or consulted with dozens of Christian organizations, such as Exodus and High Adventures Broadcasting. He also helped establish CBN's Middle East TV. In 1991 he and his wife, Susan, established Creative Resources, Inc., a Christian consulting and public relations firm. It provides opportunities for communication, growth and development to individuals and organizations by broadening or stimulating public exposure to resources that strengthen Christian values and ideas. It has promoted the PBS series on Bill Bennett's *Adventures in the Book of Virtues,* the CBS series *Christy* and the Family Channel's *Ditchdigger's Daughters.*

Don has written articles on ethics, deception, management and the media for such publications as *Charisma, Religious Broadcasting* and *New Man.* He is also the author of *Keeping Fit,* a book that encourages Christians to take care of their health. He has scaled mountains on three continents, including the Matterhorn in Switzerland.

The Otises have three boys and live near Sandpoint, Idaho.